From Beethoven to Bill Evans:

WESTERN HARMONY SIMPLIFIED

by Tom Regis

© Tom Regis, 2011

This book is dedicated to my mom, Lani Regis, whose piano renditions of Beethoven's Sonata Pathetique, Chopin's Fantasie Impromptu, and Bumble Bee Boogie, struck me as great forces of nature while in my formative years. She also pushed me just hard enough . . .

ACKNOWLEDGMENTS

I want to express my great appreciation to Joseph Maneri, who made the study of classical harmony fun and inspiring, Nevarte Adriane, my beloved childhood piano teacher, Charlie Banacos who pulled my jazz chops and understanding together, and Ran Blake for introducing me to music I hadn't heard, and for encouraging my inner voice. A special thanks also goes out to Bernie Sirelson, who proved that you can make great connections through Craigslist. Bernie was instrumental in turning my keyboard graphic sketches into reality, untangling my Sibelius files, and typesetting and formatting the book – all this with a great vibe and work ethic.

And, of course, I can't forget Beethoven and Bill Evans, and those in between, the conduits of organized sound who help us to feel the depth, soul, and life of music.

From Beethoven to Bill Evans:

WESTERN HARMONY SIMPLIFIED

by Tom Regis

© Tom Regis, 2011

Contents

CHAPTER 1: INTRODUCTION 8

- USE OF PIANO 9
- A NOTE ON THE INCLUDED COMMENTS 10
- USING THE APPENDICES 11
- WRITER'S BACKGROUND 12
- THE BROAD OUTLINE OF THE FUNDAMENTALS OF THE SYSTEM 16

CHAPTER II: DIATONIC HARMONY 19

- KEYS and DIATONICISM 22
- THE C MAJOR DIATONIC SCALE SYSTEM 24
- THE I, IV and V CHORDS 31
- TENSION AND RELEASE – MUSICAL ATTRACTION 33

CHAPTER III: THE SEVENTH CHORD 37

- NUMERICAL IDENTIFIERS 37
- SHARPS AND FLATS 39
- INTERVALS 40
- EXPANDING THE ROLE OF THE V7 49
- BACK FROM INTERVAL LAND 53

CHAPTER IV: INTRODUCING NON-DIATONIC NOTES AND 2 NEW SCALES 54

THE NOTE F#, THE D7 CHORD AND THE G MAJOR SCALE 54
THE NOTE Bb, THE C7 CHORD AND THE F MAJOR SCALE 56
REVIEWING THE SEVENTH CHORD 58

CHAPTER V: EXPANSION 62

THE II V I SEQUENCE - COMMON PATTERNS IN HARMONY 62
THE II V I - - IMPLICATIONS AND EXTRAPOLATIONS (The V of the V)... 66
DISCRETIONARY DOMINANT CHORDS 68
MORE ON THE V7 TO V7 CHORD, DISCRETIONARY CHORDS AND THE POWER OF THE 3RD AND 7th NOTE OF THE CHORD 69
TRITONE SUBSTITUTION CHORDS 73

CHAPTER VI: THE SUSPENDED CHORD 79

THE "SUS" CHORD 79
THE SUS CHORD AND DISCRETION 83

CHAPTER VII: THE MINOR DIATONIC SYSTEM 87

THE THREE MINOR SCALES 87
THE USE OF DISCRETION IN THE MINOR DIATONIC SYSTEM 91
BLACK ORPHEUS CHORD "CHANGES" 96

CHAPTER VIII: INSIDE AND OUTSIDE THE DIATONIC SYSTEM 99

COLORING CHORDS WITH DIATONIC CHORD EXTENSIONS 99

ALTERED CHORDS – USING NON-DIATONIC EXTENSION NOTES TO CREATE DEEPER COLORS AND A HIGHER DEGREE OF TENSION AND RELEASE 104

CHAPTER IX: THE BLUES – WHERE THE DOMINANT IS KING 116

THE BLUES SCALE 117
THE BLUES AND THE DIATONIC 122

CHAPTER X: MODES 129

FORMING NEW TONAL CENTERS FROM THE MAJOR SCALE 129
MODES - A NEW APPROACH TO CHORD FORMATION AND COLORING 132
MODES AND THE STANDARD JAZZ VOICINGS 140
A WORD ON CLUSTERS 142

CHAPTER XI: OTHER EXPANDED APPROACHES 147

SYMMETRY AND SHAPE 147
II V MOVEMENT, MODULATIONS, AND NEO-SOUL 154
FOLK CHORDING 158
DIMINISHED AND AUGMENTED CHORDS – "THE VAGRANT CHORDS" 162
  The Diminished Chord 162
  The Augmented Chord 166
POLYCHORDS AND PEDAL POINTS 170
  Polychords 171
  Pedal Points 175

CHAPTER XII: CLOSING THOUGHTS 178

APPENDICES 182

      Staff Notation for the Non-Reader...183

1.   Formation of Triads...186
2.   Voice Movement Between Triads 190
3.   Formation of Seventh Chords 194
4.   Voice Movement Between Seventh Chords 200
5.   Intervals...203
6.   The Use of Discretion and Substitution Chords 208
7.   Formation of the Suspended Chord...213
8.   The Minor Diatonic System 217
9.   Diatonic Extensions and the Standard Jazz Voicings........................224
10. Altered Jazz Chords 235
11. The Blues 241
12. Modes and Modal Chording..250
13. Diminished and Augmented Chords 254
14. Polychords and Pedal Points 261

FROM BEETHOVEN TO BILL EVANS: WESTERN HARMONY SIMPLIFIED

CHAPTER 1: INTRODUCTION

This book will present harmony – the sounding and organization of notes played simultaneously or in sequence with a vertical relationship – in as simple and straight forward a manner as possible. The presentation will start with the fundamentals and continue into the widening world of harmony as seen through the expansive lens of jazz. The book is written for the novice musician, even those entirely unfamiliar with the language of music, as well as for the advanced musician. Concepts are presented in a step by step approach, with great care taken to not omit any crucial links. This is an attempt to be sensitive to the frustration that inevitably occurs when an instruction manual leaves out an important link in the chain of understanding. Hopefully, this will be of great help to the novice. The book also presents harmony (or at least one musician's view of harmony) in a way that presents a seemingly complex subject as a unified whole. As well as being helpful to the novice, this should also be of great value to the advanced performer or composer.

As you will see, most of the analysis and examples provided in this book are presented in the key of C[1] Essentially, this is done for the purpose of simplification. Having noted this, it's also important to mention that for a musician to develop fully, he or she must eventually learn to play and think fluidly in all keys. It would be wise for the more intermediate and advanced

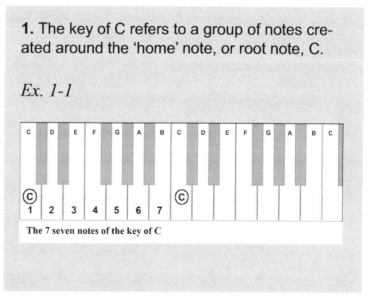

1. The key of C refers to a group of notes created around the 'home' note, or root note, C.

Ex. 1-1

The 7 seven notes of the key of C

musicians to pursue this task while learning the concepts in this book. There are various books with exercises addressing this need, however, the material here should provide the means at least indirectly, to work through these other keys. This will become clearer as we proceed through this analysis.

Also for the purpose of simplification, this book will present concepts and technical/theoretical information only as it is required. Often, harmony is presented by providing so much foundational information that the learning process can become overly burdensome. The approach of this book is to prioritize the overall system and present details in as non-cumbersome a way as possible. What is asked of the reader is that each concept be digested as there is a conscious attempt here to facilitate an understanding block by block. It is accordingly <u>better to move slowly than try to absorb too much</u> – be patient, there is a 'method to the madness.'

USE OF PIANO

Understanding that there will be readers of this book who play a variety of instruments, I have to say categorically - it is highly preferable that musicians use a piano for the study of harmony. It is no accident conservatories require students of every instrument type to base their harmony studies on piano. Piano is the instrument where the notes are most readily available for view and the scale systems repeat in visible symmetrical patterns;[2] it is the instrument that is fully polyphonic;[3] and, it is the instrument with a range

2. A scale is a group of notes that comprise a key.

Ex. 1-2

7 notes of the C scale

that spans all instruments of the symphonic orchestra from contra basses to the highest piccolo flute. The good news is that studying piano in the context of the lessons presented here is simple. First, most of the illustrations in this book are presented in a keyboard format, rather than in the more typically used staff and note format. Second, as we will be focusing on the key of C, we will primarily be looking at the white notes of the keyboard – the black notes will surface periodically, but only in context of our basic white note scale. Finally, although piano has 88 total notes, because the seven note scales recur in symmetrical patterns, our study is simplified accordingly.

> **3.** Polyphony refers to 2 or more notes played simultaneously as opposed to monophony which refers to a single voiced melody line.

Ex. 1-3

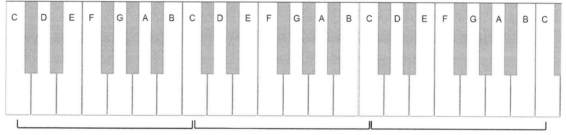

Same pattern of notes repeats in sequence

A NOTE ON THE INCLUDED COMMENTS

It is essential that the reader take the time to read the boxed comments used frequently within this book. Most often, the comments are not merely references or anecdotes but contain lessons, steps, or definitions necessary for the immediate understanding of a principle or a bridge to a related concept. The comments have also been used as a means of maintaining a unity in the discussions. At times, it may be necessary to explain a given point, but doing so in the body of the text would create too much of a detour. So, take the time to absorb the information; think of reading the comments as a constructive mini-vacation from the sequential text. Hopefully this will be a pleasant diversion.

It should also be noted that, at times, sequential paragraphs, as well as some of the comments, have been used to explore areas that may not directly link to the immediate discussion. This device is used in order to expand the inquiry to areas of interest and more advanced concepts. The goal of this book, to be sure, is to take the reader step by step, however, I do not want to limit the discussion so much by this step by step approach as to miss a larger picture. Certainly the subject of music and harmony is in the end about magic and majesty; we wouldn't want to miss this along the way.

USING THE APPENDICES

Appendices are available at the end of the book. These appendices serve two important purposes. First, you might find that as certain topics and terms recur, it may be necessary to reacquaint oneself with a definition, an outline, or a chart. Many of the appendices provide this summary material. While initial explanations will be provided in the body of the text, the quick and easy tabbing should encourage the reader to reinforce his or her understanding as required. Take the time to use this supplementary information. A second purpose of the appendices is to provide the reader the opportunity to work more deeply on a particular subject. While one can primarily read this book as an overview, in order to gain a wider understanding and develop fluency, specific detailed work may be required. The appendices provide this study material. As a bonus, the appendices are in large part presented in an immediately 'readable' staff note format allowing the student without this skill to begin developing facility in this area. The reader can work according to his or her own level with or without the help of a teacher.

WRITER'S BACKGROUND

Finally, a few words on my background might be useful in order to present a picture of the kinds of resources available to the musician seeking to further his or her training. Also, this can help to show how I arrived to see harmony as something notably simple and from there, developed the motivation to pass this understanding forward.

I began studying piano at age six and was fortunate enough to be introduced to reading music at this early age. The advantages of studying so young are obvious: children learn a new language easily and without a sense of limits (perhaps except – in my case - the tears I shed over being required to practice the obligatory hour before being set free to join my fellow gridironers). In spite of my periodic angst, I was fortunate to be exposed to the great minds and spirits of the classical composers at this early age. Along with the sense of discipline and accomplishment engendered by this study, probably the greatest benefit was to be able to participate in the creation of art/music at the extraordinarily high level set out by the composers and absorb all that that entails.

> **4.** The lesson here is that there is no real shortcut for developing this familiarity. One must spend the requisite time at the keyboard. Fortunately, much of this time does not have to be in going over exercises or in the study of theory. As long as there is some understanding of the harmonic basis of your
> *(Continued)*

Through this study of classical music, I was introduced to scales and some basic theory. The most useful result of this early study was the natural familiarity I have with keys and scales. This has been of tremendous service because the various notes and scales of the keyboard are for me like the proverbial "back of the hand."[4] With respect to understanding harmony however, like many other classically trained musicians, my study and overall understanding was not comprehensive. At age 17, I took some jazz lessons and was introduced to theory on a much more comprehensive level. It became clear, then and throughout my later years of study and teaching (particularly my study with Charlie Banacos of Boston fame), that jazz training provides a more integrated approach towards conveying concepts of harmony than the ordinary classical course. Jazz pedagogy has in effect summed up the evolution of Western harmony and set it forth in a concise manner.

> material (the intent of this book), playing through tunes or improvising will go a long way towards this end.

Having noted the above, this is not to say that the classical world did not develop its own comprehensive system. It exists and predated jazz study, but it seems to not have been the focus of classical instrumental teaching, at least during the period of my education. (Perhaps this is due to the primary desire of the student and teacher to develop and perform the repertoire). Nevertheless, as a student at New England Conservatory of Music, I was fortunate enough to meet Joe Maneri, who introduced me to the Schoenberg Theory of Harmony. Arnold Schoenberg was an Austrian composer who was instrumental in moving classical music through its late Romantic period and then, in some ways, oversaw the disintegration of harmony into a systemized form of 'atonality.' Partly as a response to the natural chorus of critics he encountered, he wrote the Theory of Harmony, a book that outlined the evolution of classical music through the study of choral writing (composing for 4 voices). This system is comprehensive, starting with the earliest periods of diatonic music[5] and moving into the late romantic periods represented by Mahler and Berg.

> **5.** Diatonicism more or less refers to a harmonic system based on the notes of a given scale. This concept is an essential element of this book and will be explained in more detail further along.

Western Harmony Simplified

The importance of this system for me was threefold: first, I was able to solidify the jazz harmony training I had had and put it into the context of classical harmony, realizing that the harmonies of the two worlds (apart from the blues that inflects jazz) are essentially the same; second, by writing choral phrases modeling the evolution of classical harmony, and living with harmonic phrase movement – the way individual notes work together as chords[6] and how chords properly sequence from one to another (a concept important in jazz harmony as well), I was able to experience and be influenced by this incredible aesthetic; and finally, as Schoenberg so clearly presented the underlying structure of harmony, it became clear to me the idea of an ordered system. It is this latter point that informs the notion of this book.

> **6.** 'Chords' result from the sounding of two or more notes simultaneously.

Developing as a jazz player throughout my musical journey has also brought me greater understanding of the basic elements of harmony. Leaving out the blues element for now (addressed later), jazz incorporates the basic diatonic concepts presented throughout this book. The jazz idiom also presents numerous opportunities for working through different keys. In fact, fluency in jazz requires a thorough familiarity with keys. The movement through the different keys is facilitated by knowing the scales that comprise these keys. This facility is enhanced immeasurably by understanding the singular harmonic system upon which each of these keys is built. Another point – the improvisatory impulses of jazz also gave life to Miles Davis's idea that there are no wrong notes.[7] My take on this idea is that, at worst, one is always a half-step[8] away from a "correct" note. Even here, however, there is no wrong note as a note a half step away is inevitably drawn to the more "correct" note. This idea will be explored in greater detail in short time as is it is one of the foundational steps

> **7.** The complete statement of his idea is that what follows the note is of vital importance.

14 Western Harmony Simplified

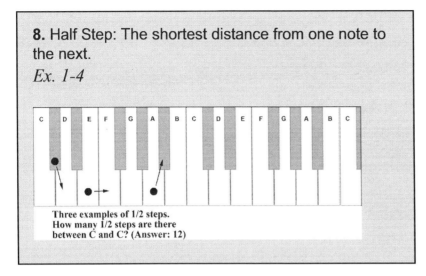

8. Half Step: The shortest distance from one note to the next.

Ex. 1-4

Three examples of 1/2 steps. How many 1/2 steps are there between C and C? (Answer: 12)

of the system presented in this book, particularly as it pertains to jazz.[9]

Another experience in my life helped me to better understand the process of learning and teaching. In 1993, I journeyed to Israel where I lived and worked for five years. During the first year of my stay, I studied Hebrew in a course provided by the government in order to help assimilate new arrivals. Towards the end of my level's program, the teacher presented all the gram-

---

9 References to jazz and jazz harmony should not bring to mind only music from the jazz repertoire. Jazz harmony has informed various styles of music including r&b, pop, rock, bossa nova, salsa, and others.

---

mar we had studied (which happened to be the totality of Hebrew grammar) in outline form on the board. It occurred to me after seeing this presentation that if I had known of this summary before we started – in other words, had been presented with the forest before the trees – the learning process would have been much easier. Back in the States while in law school a few years later, I was able to successfully incorporate this approach to learning, that is – to see the larger picture of a subject and not get lost in the details. This approach lies at the heart of the system presented in this book. Although there are individual pieces of information along the way, the book attempts to convey that harmony is a system based on fundamental concepts. That is the most important lesson to be drawn from these pages.

Western Harmony Simplified

So dear reader, in light of the above, here is the nutshell – the grammar written at the end of the course so to speak - but here, for your edification, *before* the lesson. Please don't be concerned about memorizing or understanding the whole of this summary right away. The details and definitions will be covered as we proceed. More advanced concepts will follow once the basic system is outlined. Use this summary as an initial guide before moving forward and then as a fall back when the trees start to cover the forest.

THE BROAD OUTLINE OF THE FUNDAMENTALS OF THE SYSTEM OF WESTERN HARMONY PRESENTED IN MORE DETAIL THROUGHOUT THE BOOK ARE AS FOLLOWS:

1)   Harmony is built upon a 7 note scale either major or minor.

2)   Seven sequential triadic chords[10] (chords containing 3 notes) are contained within this scale, each one serving a role, some more dominant than others.

---

10. Remember, a chord is formed by notes sounding together.

---

3)   The triadic chords can be expanded into larger chords, the most common being the four note chord, also comprised of notes from the scale. This chord is referred to as a "seventh" chord.

4)   The first chord (the I chord) is considered the home (or tonic) chord, it is based on the first note of the scale; the fifth chord (the V chord), starting on the fifth note of the scale, is known as the dominant chord – a chord that often intrinsically leads back (resolves) to the home chord (I). This V

chord is often a four note chord (called a V7 chord) with the fourth note of the chord contributing to the attraction exhibited from the V chord to the I chord.

5) For all chords there is another chord that is relatively dominant that can be used as a means of arriving to that chord. These "dominant" chords function similarly to the V chord as it moves to the I chord.

6) Notes and chords a half step above a given note or chord can serve the same function as the dominant chord, that is: they are naturally inclined - magnetically pulled – towards the note or chord a half step below or above.

7) As in step 5, any chord can have a chord a half step above that serves as a quasi dominant chord to that chord.

8) Dominant chords or chords functioning like dominant chords can be used merely to arrive to a given chord within the scale or to move to a different key center altogether.

9) In addition to the chords built on a given scale (steps 1-3), jazz harmony is built in large part from the concepts outlined in steps 5-8.

10) Concepts used in jazz and popular music, including the II V I and other progressions, suspended chords, the upper structure of chords, modes, blues and composing or playing "outside the key," are derived from or are strongly related to the basic diatonic system.

11) Once the diatonic system is understood, it can be transposed to all 12 keys with no additional conceptual steps required.

12) All of the above concepts can be applied to the major scale's relative minor scale which is derived from the note materials of the major scale.

For sure, there is more to learning harmony and the vast array of available musical colors than is contained within the short outline above. This book will reference and explain some of these potentials, certainly the ones that are integral or at least peripherally important to the system as a whole. Again, the outline above is useful to gain a sense of the wider picture.

CHAPTER II: DIATONIC HARMONY

Starting out, we will take a look at harmony from the perspective of its most basic components. Western harmony, that is, tonal music from Europe and the Western hemisphere, contains a twelve note sequence which repeats itself an "octave" either above or below, depending on whether the movement is ascending or descending. These twelve notes have been given letter names from A through G.[11]

> **11.** The detectives among you may be wondering how the 12 note sequence can be comprised of 7 consecutive notes represented by the letter names: A, B, C, D, E, F, G. The answer, which will be discussed in more detail later, lies in the simple use of tones called sharps and flats that fall in between these 7 tones.

Ex. 2-1

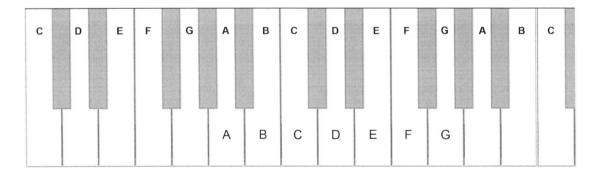

A new "octave" occurs at the end of each twelve note sequence. In this new octave range, the twelve specific tones in the sequence will sound higher or lower in pitch. However, other than the sense of higher and lower pitch, the tones/notes in each octave which bear the same letter name of the tone in the previous octave share the same tonal center.

Ex. 2-2

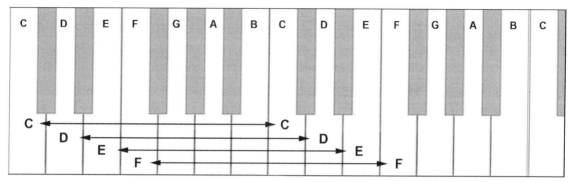

**Notes with the same letter name 12 notes apart
share the same tonal center and are called "octaves"**

The astounding effect of notes an octave apart is that these notes sound as if they come from the same home. The Harvard dictionary describes this relationship as "the most perfect consonance." On a technical level, the tone/note labeled "A" towards the middle of a piano keyboard produces a sound wave that vibrates at a frequency of 440 times per second. The "A" one octave above vibrates at a frequency of 880 times per second. This two to one relationship among tones an octave apart is unvarying.

Ex. 2-3

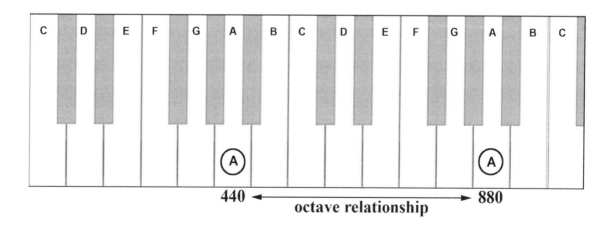

This phenomenon of the interrelationship of tones that ascend or descend and then repeat in a sequence that sounds the same as the previous sequence, leads one to the question: how can tones move up or down and still arrive at essentially the same place? It is as if you climbed or descended a mountain and kept arriving at the same place in some sort of noticeable sequential pattern. Every half mile, for example, you might see an exact representation, perhaps of different scale, of some unique visual previously encountered.

The mathematical relationship of these tones noted above, though perhaps informative of some underlying science, in the end can only add to the wonderment. Philosophers ranging from Aristotle to Gurdjieff have examined this phenomenon and their views, while well worth looking at, are not quite fitting for the scope of this inquiry. Suffice it to say that, for our purposes, we will see that the magical existence of the octave[12] greatly simplifies the process of understanding the relationship of tones. Imagine if we had to look at the interrelationships of all 88 notes of a piano keyboard; the task would be impossible in its complexity. In our case, our inquiry has been reduced and limited to twelve notes and then primarily the seven note scale. Once we understand how Western harmony has organized these tones, our task will have more or less been completed.[13]

> 12 The Harvard Dictionary of Music states that, for the octave, "no convincing explanation has ever been found."

> **13.** This idea of man organizing tones into a harmony system raises a chicken or the egg question: was it man who organized these tones, or has the natural law of sound, the natural laws of harmony prevailed, causing man only to discover the inevitable?

KEYS and DIATONICISM

Fortunately, the concept of "keys," while initially presenting a hurdle, significantly reduces the work required for our understanding of harmony. A *key* refers to the home tone of a given piece of music. In most music that the Western (and even non-Western) ear is familiar with, there is a tonal center to the music; this tonal center is often used as the last (and sometimes the first) note of the musical piece. Beethoven's 5th symphony famously starting with – da da da daaaa, is an example of Beethoven purposely creating a sense of confusion - of not being settled with the key. On the other hand, in classical music, including the works of Beethoven, there is typically a great last chord, a moment where everything has arrived; this is the key, the tonal center.

If we look at the white notes of a piano, we can quickly understand the concept of a "key." The white notes of a piano starting on the "middle C" of the keyboard and ascending are C, D, E, F, G A, B and again C through B. These seven notes starting on C make up what is called the C major scale. Since, for now, we will not be introducing any notes outside of this scale, by definition, this scale and any music we make with it will be considered **diatonic**. Understanding diatonicism is important because this idea that music – the melody and harmony - is derived from the notes of a scale is the foundation to understanding all of Western music.

In the analysis to follow, we will be using the tone C and its diatonic scale C,D,E,F,G,A,B as the key. The C tone will be the home note – the *tonic*, the note that seems most familiar and at rest to our ears. However, before going further in our diatonic examination of the Key of C, let's step back for a moment and talk about the notes we left out. In addition to the seven white notes of the keyboard, there are five black notes – C sharp(#), D#, F#, G#, and A#.[14]

14. These notes are also also referred to as flat notes (i.e. D flat(b) instead of C#) depending on which key is utilizing the notes. This idea will be examined in more detail later in this study.

Ex. 2-4

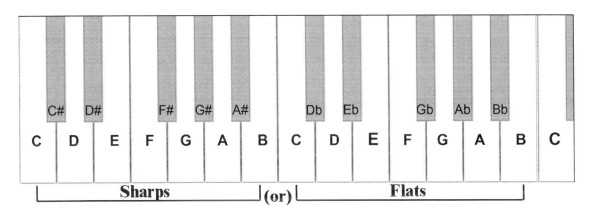

Each of these twelve notes can be the tonal center for its own major scale.[15] While for the performing musician, each different key may bring with it physical challenges, the good news is that the organization of harmony within one key is entirely applicable to all other keys. In other words, once harmony is understood within one key, harmony will be understood in all twelve keys. Now, more on C major.

15. Practically every major classical composer wrote music in each of the 12 keys. In the popular music world, Bob Marley's "No Woman No Cry" was written in the key of C, while Paul McCartney's "Yesterday" was written in the Key of F. Keys are often chosen to evoke a particular emotional color (C major has a purity about it, almost a softness, while E major has brightness and boldness, almost a metallic edge). A key may also be chosen out of the practical necessity of suiting a vocalist's or instrumentalist's musical range.

THE C MAJOR DIATONIC SCALE SYSTEM

The C major scale system – C,D,E,F,G,A,B,C – can be organized using a simple numerical system (mathophobes need not be concerned). C is 1 (or the first note of the scale), D is 2, E 3, F 4, G 5, A 6, and B 7.[16]

> **16.** Although the letter names of the notes range from A to G, the C major scale beginning on the note C is the first scale taught due to its simplicity. (The scale contains all white notes.)

Ex. 2-5

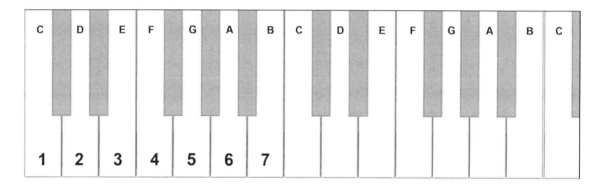

This number system is used as much or more than the individual letters within musical discourse. It is also this system that enables us to translate our understanding of one key into all 12 keys. Notice that these notes are the white notes of the piano keyboard.

To this point, we have discussed the individual notes that comprise the key. These notes can be used to create melodies, the musical expression which is the basis of a song. A melody is considered "monophonic" because typically in the melody, only one note is sounded at a time, as in a human voice or a saxophone. As we will be working in the key of C, any melody from this scale would be considered a diatonic melody in the key of C. In addition, the diatonic scale also provides the material (the notes) that allow for the simultaneous sounding of notes, referred to a "chords." For now, just think of melodies and chords within a diatonic system as being inextricably linked – the chords provide the material for the melodies as much as the melodies provide the material for the chords. It is the different chords that are formed within the diatonic system and how they move within this system that is the main focus of this book. We will see later that melodies can become part of the chords, but for now we will be analyzing harmony by focusing on the formation of chords and chord movement.

We can build chords in the key of C major by using the scale notes of the C major scale. The most common and basic chords are the three note major and minor chords, also referred to as major or minor triads. The beauty of our C major white note scale is that it becomes very easy to visualize and play chords on a piano. A series of three notes, two apart in the white note scale form the major and minor triads. For example: the C, E, and G form a C major triad (derived from the scale: **CDEFGABC**).

Ex. 2-6

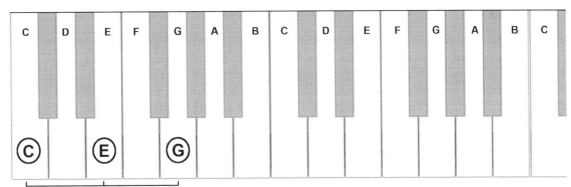

These three notes form the C <u>major</u> chord

The D, F, and A played together form a D minor triad (derived from the scale: **CDEFGABC**).

Ex. 2-7

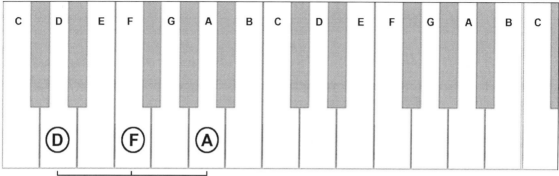

These three notes form the D minor chord

Using this process, the remaining chords coming out of the C major scale are E minor, F major, G major, A minor, and B diminished.

Ex. 2-8[17]

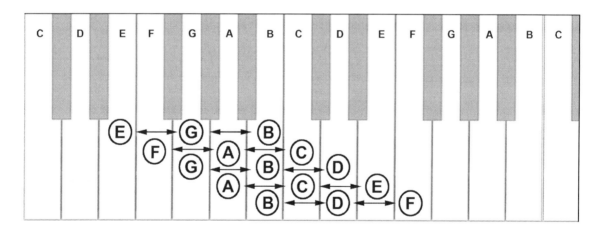

The above descriptions and comment 17 cover the most basic formation of the major and minor triads. In these examples, the chords are in the "root" position, that is – the bottom note of the chord is the tonal center (**C** (tonal center), E, G).

26   Western Harmony Simplified

17. THE FORMATION OF MAJOR, MINOR, AND DIMINISHED CHORDS

In the graphic below, you will see there are a different number of "half steps" between the notes C and E, and E and G. (A half step is a move from one tone to its nearest neighbor.) A distance of four half steps (as between the C and E) is called a major third "interval"; a distance of three half steps (as between the E and G) is called a minor third "interval." (An interval is a common term in music theory and practice that refers to the distance between notes.)

Ex. 2-9

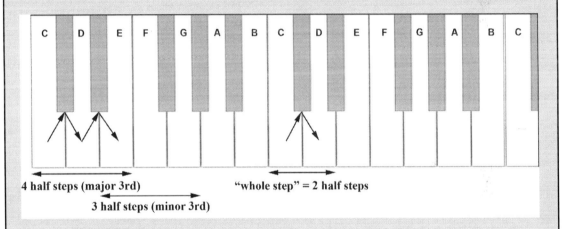

If you play these 'intervals' on the keyboard, you will notice that the major and minor third intervals have a different sound – the major third generally evokes a more bright mood and the minor third a more somber tone. What's most important for this inquiry is that learning the difference in the formation of the major and minor third intervals allows us to understand the structural formation of major, minor and diminished triads.

(continued)

Accordingly: a ***major triad* is formed** by building from the first note an interval of a major third followed by a minor third; a ***minor triad* is formed** from an interval of a minor third followed by a major third; a ***diminished triad* is formed** from an interval of a minor third followed by a minor third.

Ex. 2-10

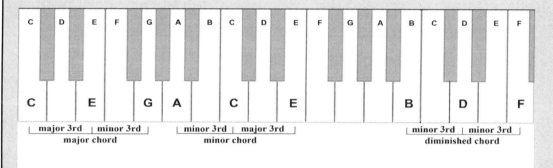

We will cover the topic of intervals in more detail later on, but it is useful here to point out that the third note of the triad (i.e., the G in the C major chord) is an interval of a fifth from the C. Keep this in mind for later.

Ex. 2-11

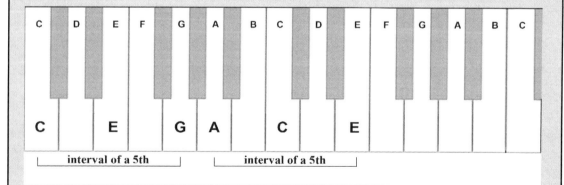

This first/bottom note is most often the note a bass player or other low range supporting instrument would play in an ensemble as the chord is sounded. Having said this, it is also *crucial to understand* that music is not limited to root position chords. In piano pedagogy, the triads are initially taught as block chords – first, the root position (CEG), then the triad in "first" position (EGC) and "second" position (GCE). (Please see Appendix 1 Formation of Triads for review and further study.)

Ex. 2-12

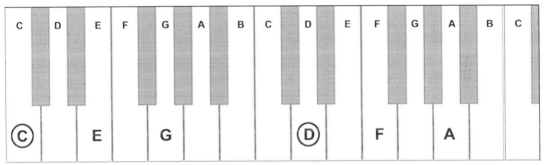

C is the root of the C major chord   D is the root of the D minor chord

The C, E, G that comprise the C major chord for example can also be incorporated anywhere within the range of an instrument. One could play an E, G, and C in that order to make the sound of a C major chord. The classical composers often would place the notes of a triad in different instruments and ranges to affect a sound and particular emotion. For example, the basses, cellos and tubas might play a G as the bottom note, the violas, horns and clarinets an E in the middle range, and the violins, flutes, and oboe a C as the highest note. Some of these notes could also be 'doubled,' an octave apart. This way, a seemingly simple chord - C major – can be painted with an array of colors and shapes.

Western Harmony Simplified

Ex. 2-13

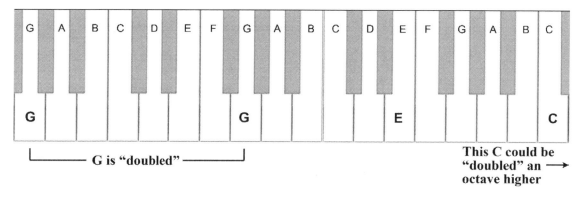

Likewise, a guitar sounds a C major chord in its own warmly unique and pleasing way - the notes getting scrambled and sometimes doubled to achieve a droning folk effect. What's most important about learning the basic triad in root position is that this position is easy to visualize and quickly facilitates a familiarity with the basic components of chords. This foundation can then be expanded upon.

Now, again, returning to our home - the C major scale. This scale contains seven triads: C major, D minor, E minor, F major, G major, A minor and B diminished. Just as the individual notes of the scale are assigned numbers, the chords within the scale are also given numerical identifiers, in this case, Roman numerals, sometimes referred to as 'degrees.' C (major) is the I chord (or first degree), D minor the II chord, E minor the III chord, F the IV chord, G the V chord, A minor the VI chord, and B diminished the VII chord.[18]

> **18.** Chords with no designation of major or minor default to the major chord. A C chord is to be read as C major. An F chord – F major. This is merely a convenient shorthand used commonly in the professional music world and will be used for the remainder of this book.

Ex. 2-14

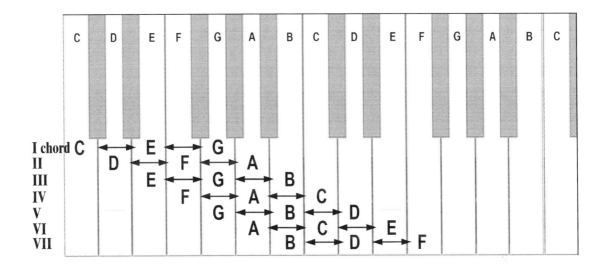

While all of the above chords are used within Western musical styles from the most complex to the more simple forms of these chords, it is the I chord (C), the IV chord (F), and the V chord (G) that most clearly provide the foundation for Western music and prompt deeper inquiry.

THE I, IV and V CHORDS

Music is essentially the movement of sound through time. If sound remains static, having no destination, no journey so to speak, there would be nothing of interest to keep our attention. Similarly, if sound moves endlessly in random variations with no sense of organization or purpose, we would also at some point lose interest. The I, IV, and V chords provide an immediate destination for our musical sojourns; they act as guideposts and are the essential first steps in our Western musical journeys. Their power is such that whole genres of music have functioned using only these chords. Even as music becomes more harmonically complex, in most cases it remains structurally bound directly or indirectly to the I, IV, and V chords.

The power and primacy of the I chord is easy to see (and hear). The I chord is home; it can provide a starting and ending point and a welcome stopping off point in between. Our musical journeys need the I chord; it provides stability and a sense of security as well as a jumping off point into greater adventure. If the function of this I chord is so apparent, what gives the IV and V chords their importance? The simple answer may be that, accepting that the I chord is primary (C in our example), F (IV) and G (V) are chords that have the strongest connection, an almost magnetic attraction, to or from our primary root chord C.

Fortunately for our inquiry, there is a both scientific and musical basis for the above thesis, that is - the inherent attractions binding the C (I), F (IV) and G (V) chords.[19] On the material level, individual tones derived from most musical instruments contain a fundamental pitch (the intended note) as well as a series of overtones that, while not immediately apparent to the ear, have an intrinsic effect. Taking the note C as an example: the first three overtones above this fundamental are the C an octave above the fundamental C, and the G and C two octaves above the fundamental. Similarly, taking the note F as an example: the first three overtones above this fundamental F are the octave above F, the C and an F two octaves above and on through the rest of the series. In effect, the note C has a G (C's second overtone) as part of its basic makeup just as the F has a C (F's second overtone) as part of its basic tonal makeup. The fundamental G of the G note is of course closely tied to the C note by way of the C's second overtone G. In short, the result of these overlapping fundamentals and overtones between the first, fourth and fifth notes of the scale is a tonal commonality. In a manner of speaking, among these tones (and the chords built upon them), you are never far away from home.

> **19.** Remember: these numerical distinctions will apply to all 12 keys!

Ex. 2-15[20]

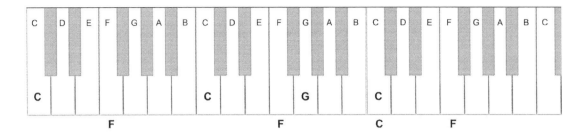

> **20.** The fourth overtone in the series from the fundamental C is E. The C, G and E notes inherent in the fundamental C form the notes of the C major chord, the first chord in the diatonic system!

TENSION AND RELEASE – MUSICAL ATTRACTION

As indicated earlier, in addition to the commonality of tones, there is a strong magnetic pull between the I, IV and V chords. In the Key of C, the G chord is magnetically pulled towards C (V to I), and C is magnetically pulled towards F (I to IV).[21] In order to understand the musical basis for this attraction, we need to look at the design of the major scale. The C major scale (and all other major scales) is built utilizing, from the root C, Two whole steps, one half step, three whole steps and one half step (**C**, C#, **D**, D#, **E**, **F**, F#, **G**, G#, **A**, A# and **B**, **C**). The two half step movements of this scale, E to

> **21.** Not only can these magnetic relationships be seen countless times throughout the classical repertoire, but these two 2 chord "progressions" have been the basis for folk songs, funk vamps, rock grooves, blues, country swing, garage band jams, jazz intros/outros, salsa choruses, and just about every Western genre of music imaginable.

F and B to C, provide unique stress and relief points closely connected to the V -> I and the I -> IV chord relationships.

Ex. 2-16

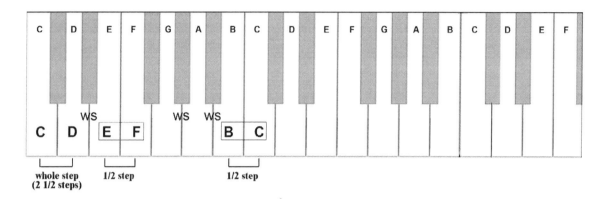

On a fundamental level, even outside the context of the relative intervals within a scale,[22] there is an inherent pull between notes a half step apart. The easiest and most convincing way to understand this is to play or sing these intervals and notice the natural inclination towards the adjacent note. This inclination is even more pronounced between the two half steps intervals within the context of the C major scale (and all other major scales!). The application of this 'attraction' to our examination of the V to I and the I to IV chord relationships is as follows: the V chord G (in our example, G-B-D) moves to the I chord C (C-E-G). The B note of the first chord G is naturally inclined to move towards the note in the scale a half step away - C. As simple as that, there is tension and relief. Similarly, the I chord (in our example, C-E-G) is drawn to the IV chord F (F-A-C) in part because the E note of the first chord C is naturally inclined to move towards the note in the scale a half step away – F. Again, natural tension and relief. The C chord is quite content to move towards the F chord.

> **22.** Remember - an interval refers to the distance between notes.

Ex. 2-17

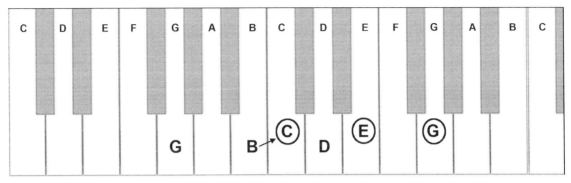

Ex. 2-18

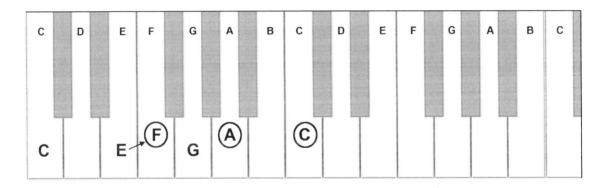

Those of you who are paying close attention or better yet tried to play the V to I and I to IV chord movements on the piano may have noticed a problem in my presentation of these progressions. Taking the V to I movement for example – I described it as follows: the G chord (G-B-D) moves to the C chord (C-E-G). The problem: if these two chords are played as described, the B note will not move to an adjacent C because the G chord is jumping straight down (or up) to the C chord shaped in its mirror image. In order for the B note of the G chord to move directly to the C note of the C chord, a different voicing[23] will be required. Here, in order to effectuate the proper inherent tension and release of the progression, the G chord (G-**B**-D) should be followed by the voicing of the C chord in the second position (G-**C**-E).

Western Harmony Simplified 35

> **23.** This was discussed earlier. Remember that the notes of a chord may be arranged in any order that suits the desired effect. In jazz terminology, the **voicing** of a chord refers to this ordering of notes.

Ex. 2-19

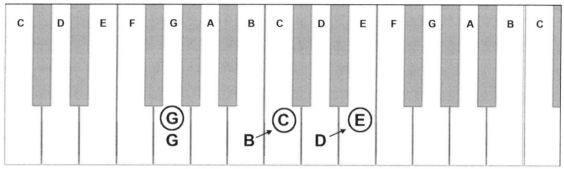

G B D of G chord moves to G C E of C chord

You can see that in this way the middle voice of the progression is able to move directly to its adjacent half step (B to C). This type of calculated movement is also described as voice leading and its importance cannot be overstated. It has been a vital part of the harmonic language all the way from Beethoven through Bill Evans, and is a technique that all arrangers and polyphonic instrumentalists must master.[24]

> **24.** Please see Appendix 2 - Voice Movement Between Triads. Time spent on this section can work wonders to develop familiarity with a key and diatonic chord movement.

CHAPTER III: THE SEVENTH CHORD

Just as we learned that the diatonic major scale can be divided into seven individual 3 note chords, it can also be divided into seven 4 note chords, called seventh chords. This is a vital concept and element of harmony, but before exploring this point further, we need to do a little housekeeping and clarify three previously mentioned subjects that will surface here again and throughout our discussions. These are: 1) the various numerical identifiers used within the harmonic system and the potential confusion this can cause; 2) the use of sharps and flats; and, 3) the concept of intervals. Please forgive this detour, but it is necessary.

NUMERICAL IDENTIFIERS

There is potential for great confusion if the various numbers used to identify elements of the harmonic system are not clarified. Up to this point, we have referred to the individual notes of the scale as the first (1st), second, third ... We have referred to the individual chords that are built from the scale as the I chord, II, III, IV ... (Again, notice here the use of Roman numerals). We have also made reference to the formation of triads and notes within each of these triads but have yet to clearly identify these individual notes numerically.

The three notes that comprise the triad are called the first (1st), the third, and the fifth of the chord. Here, there is risk of confusion for those not yet familiar with the numerical terms and their related contexts. The first, third and fifth of the triad are not the same as the first, third, and fifth of the scale. For example: the A note of the triad F-A-C that makes up the IV chord of the C major scale can be described as the 3rd of the chord F, but it is also the 6th note of the C major scale.

Ex. 3-1

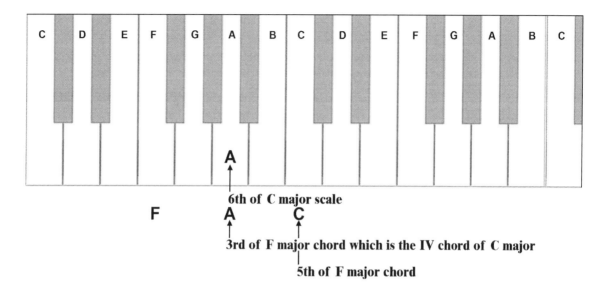

The numerical distinctions in the above example are crucial. It behooves the reader to take the time to digest this before reading further.[25] There may be further distinctions down the road that will be easier to accommodate the more solid this initial understanding.

25. The numerical identifiers of the triads (and for that matter, all the referenced identifiers) are important not only for the purpose of identification, but for the purpose of describing the sound and color associated with that note. For example: an arranger or composer may ask an instrumentalist to play a chord with the 3rd in the bass rather than the first in the bass because of the particular color and shape elicited by this voicing.

SHARPS AND FLATS

In our case, using the C major scale (the white notes of the keyboard) as our harmonic home, we can avoid dealing with the black notes for much of our discussion. However, in order to set out the harmonic system of this book we will need to incorporate them to some extent. Accordingly – you will need to understand the use of sharps and flats. The concept, discussed earlier in the book, is quite simple: if one takes any note and moves a half step above that note, the resulting note is considered a sharp note (#). For example: the note a half step above C is called C sharp. Similarly, if one takes any note and moves a half step below that note, the resulting note is considered a flat note (b). For example: the note a half step below D is called D flat.

Ex. 3-2

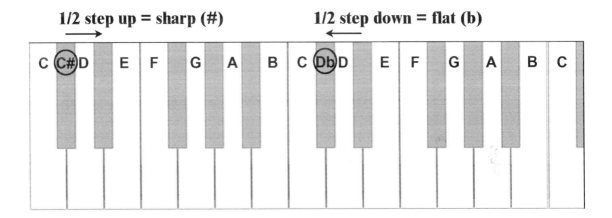

Those with detective brains may notice that C# and Db turn out to be the same note. While it is true that, while in sound, these are the same notes, there is a distinction to be made. A detailed discussion of this distinction is beyond the scope of this book. For our present purposes, we can now feel comfortable identifying the black notes as this becomes necessary. We have the **C**, **C#** (also can be named Db), **D**, **D#** (Eb), **E**, **F**, **F#** (Gb), **G**, **G#** (Ab), **A**, **A#** (Bb) and **B**, **C**.

Ex. 3-3

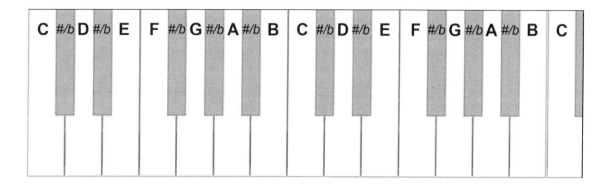

INTERVALS

Also relevant to the issue of numerical identifiers, we need to discuss one other important subject: the interval. As defined in comment 22, an interval refers to the distance between two notes. Intervals can be described using the half step as a measuring tool.

C to C# is an interval of a minor 2nd comprised of one half step;
C to D is an interval of a 2nd (or a whole step) comprised of two half steps;
C to Eb is a interval of a minor 3rd comprised of three half steps;
C to E is an interval of a 3rd (or major third) comprised of four half steps;
C to F is an interval of a 4th comprised of five half steps;
C to F# is an interval of a tritone (or a sharp 4 or flat 5) comprised of six half steps;
C to G is an interval of a 5th comprised of seven half steps;
C to Ab is an interval of a minor 6 comprised of eight half steps;
C to A is an interval of a 6th (or major 6) comprised of nine half steps;
C to Bb is an interval of a 7th comprised of ten half steps; and,
C to B is an interval of a major 7th comprised of 11 half steps.
<u>Counting these intervals as they descend works the same way</u>: C down to B would be called a minor second (or a half step) interval; C down to Bb would be called a second and so forth.

Ex. 3-4

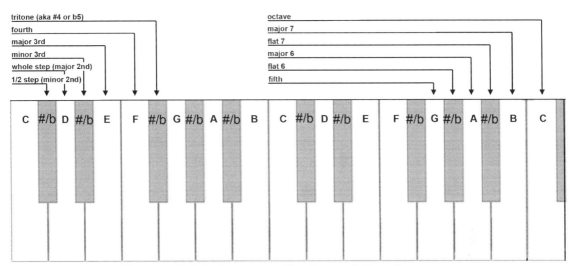

Also available in appendix for quick reference

Again – notice there is potential for confusion here because of the numerical jargon. Intervals are often referred to with their numerical distinctions, i.e., "that note is a fourth away" (describing G's distance from the D below for example). This "fourth" reference in this context is not the same as referring to the IV chord or the 4th note of the scale or as we will see shortly, the fourth note of a chord. Yes, this is a lot to chew but again, being heads up about these distinctions is important. These distinctions will increasingly become clearer and given context as we apply them to the C major diatonic system.

Before getting back to the topic at hand - the 7th chord - as a muscle building exercise in intervals and numerical identifiers, see if the following makes sense: the A note (the 6th note of the C major scale) is a 5th interval from the D note (the 2nd note of the C major scale); The B note (the 7th note of the C major scale) is a 3rd interval from the G note (the 5th note of the C major scale). The E note is a minor third interval *below* G and is an interval of a 5th above the A below and a fourth below the A above.

Western Harmony Simplified   **41**

Ex. 3-5

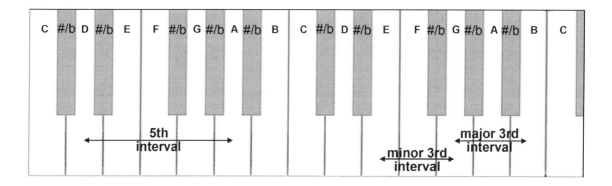

Got that? Now finally, and not least important, as in all of our study, the end point is the music that harmony evokes. Intervals are the very substance of harmony, they provide the colors of chords as well as being integral to shaping melody (when played as individual notes). For this reason, it is vital for the musician to be able to hear and recognize intervals, and ultimately to have an intuitive 'feel' for the colors they create.[26]

> **26.** To get a sense of the intrinsic differences between intervals, sing the first 2 notes of Bernstein's "Somewhere" from the musical West Side Story ("*There's a* place for us ..."), an ascending 7th interval, compared with the children's ditty "Do Re Mi," where the interval between Do and Mi is a major third – clearly these are different shapes, feelings, musical colors ... Please refer to the intervals appendix for a list of songs that correlate with ascending and descending intervals as well as for additional study and review.

Now, finally – back to the 7th chord. This chord is simple: it is merely the three note triad with an additional note added. This added note is a minor third above the third note of the triad in the root position. Using the V chord of the C major scale, the G chord G-B-D, we simply add the F to turn the

G into a G7 chord. (Notice that the F note is a diatonic note in the C major scale.)

Ex. 3-6

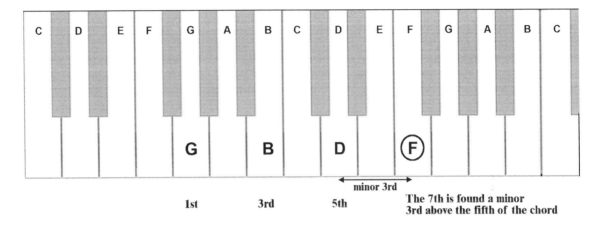

There are additional ways to derive the seventh of this G chord: first, as was noted in the explanation of intervals, the seventh interval is ten half steps above a given note; and, second, the 7th is a step down (two half steps) from the octave above the given note. In our case of using the G chord, one would simply find the seventh of this chord by taking the original G, going up an octave, and then taking a step down to find the F.

Ex. 3-7

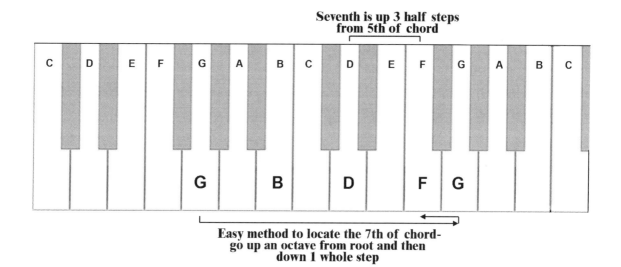

This latter method may be the easiest of all because it is very easy to visualize the octave and then move a step below that (certainly easier than counting 10 half steps up). Overall, with practice and experience, locating the seventh or any other interval for that matter will become second nature; the laborious processes will become a thing of the past.

Notice again that numbers are being applied to the G chord: the 5th of the chord is D, the 7th is F, the G is the first note. I can't overstate or remind the reader too much about the different uses of the numbering systems and the possibility for confusion. To review and practice again: The G chord is the V chord in the key of C, F is the IV chord; the note B is the seventh note in the C scale; the note F is the seventh of the G7 chord but the fourth note of the C scale; the note E is the third note of the C major scale, an interval of a 3rd from the C below it but an interval of a 5th from the A below. What interval is G from the E immediately below?[27]

27. A _minor_ third (separated by 3 half steps), distinguished from the major third which is separated by 4 half steps. This was a bit of a trick question because on the face of the keyboard, the distance between C and the E above it, and the E and the G above the E, appears the same, at least from the perspective of the white notes. What makes the difference however, is there are two black notes between C and E as opposed to one black note between the E and G. The number of half steps is therefore different within these two intervals.

Ex. 3-8

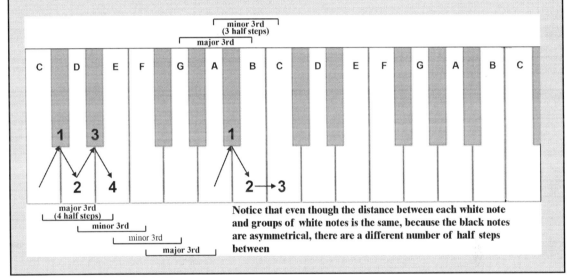

Now that we have the knowledge of and means to form the G7 chord – the questions remain, what is the significance of this chord, what, if any purpose does it serve? Simply, what essentially defines and gives purpose to the V7 chord is its power to set up the resolution to the home chord (I) – the tonic. If we think of the power and need for a home chord, the chord that provides the foundation of our tones, we can see that a chord taking us back home serves a critical purpose. In fact, the power of the V7 is such that the classical world labeled it as the "dominant" chord.

Western Harmony Simplified   45

It will help our understanding of the power of this dominant chord (V7) -> tonic chord (I) relationship to take a look at the voice movement between the two chords. We originally discussed the power of the half step relationship and how, especially in the context of a scale (C in our case), the E a half step away from the F pulls strongly towards that note as does the B towards the C a half step above. But here is what's new: the pull between half steps, depending on context, can work in either direction. In the C major diatonic scale system, the F note can have a very strong attraction to the E below. Applying this to the notes of the G7 chord, GBDF, (the V7 chord) as it moves to the C chord, GCE (the I chord), we see there are two points of strong attraction between these two chords. The B and F of the G7 chord move towards the C and E of the C chord respectively. (The B moves up to C and the F moves down to E.)

Ex. 3-9

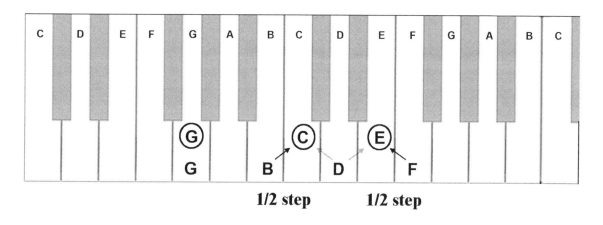

The tendencies of these notes to pull towards the other especially in the context of the G7 to C chord sequence becomes very apparent if you listen to the sequence on the keyboard. This tendency can be demonstrated even more clearly by playing only the F and B of the G7 chord and moving to the adjacent E and C notes of the C chord. Here, you can hear the strong dissonance of this F and B 'chord' and its need for resolution,[28] a need met by the movement to the E and C notes.

> **28.** For a period of time prior to the early Classical period, the tritone interval (i.e., B to F) was referred to as the Devil's interval because of its strong dissonance. It eventually became accepted particularly as it provided a powerful tension/resolution mechanism.

It needs to be noted here that there are different types of seventh chords that can be structured on the varied chord degrees of the diatonic scale. In other words, all of the diatonic chords in the C major scale (and subsequently for all major scales) can be and often are expanded into seventh chords. In fact, while the harmony of folk and rock music tends to be based more on the use of diatonic triads, much of popular music, including jazz, r&b, salsa, motown, and blues primarily use seventh chords. To explain in more detail: as we have already seen, in a diatonic system, each chord uses only notes from the given scale. In our example of the C major scale, expanding the diatonic triadic into four note seventh chords produces the following: C major7 or I maj 7 (CEGB), D minor 7/ IImin7 (DFAC), E minor 7/III min7 (EGBD), F major 7/IV maj 7 (FACE), G7 dominant/ V7 (GBDF), A minor 7/VI min 7 (ACEG), B half diminished 7/VII half dim 7 (BDFA).[29] Each of these chords is formed by adding a diatonic note a minor or major third above the fifth note of the diatonic chord.

> **29.** A diminished chord is built on intervals only of minor thirds. A true B diminished 7 would be BDF**Ab**. In order to keep this chord diatonic, the A note is used. This chord is called a half diminished or a min7b5 chord.

Western Harmony Simplified 47

Ex. 3-10

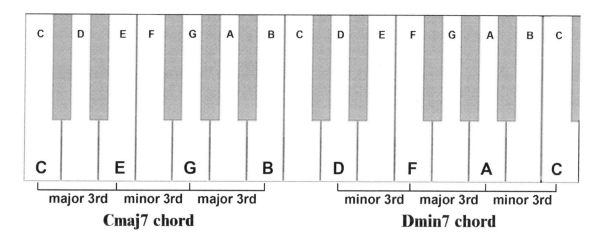

Ex. 3-11

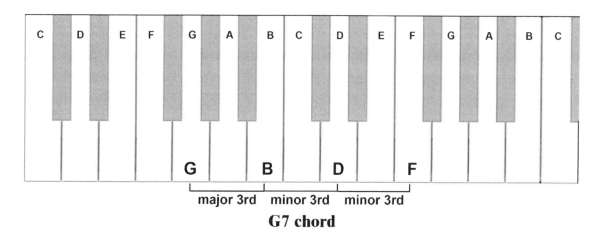

If you have access to a keyboard, play through the chords and notice the difference between the sounds of the dominant 7, major 7, and the minor 7. The dominant 7 chord has a particular bite to it, the major 7 a sort of open feeling, and the minor 7 chord a certain darkness and gravitas, but somehow still aesthetically pleasing and even calming. Significantly, you might have noticed that within the diatonic system, the V7 chord, the chord with the strongest harmonic bite, is the only dominant chord among the seven seventh chords. Because of the layout of the major scale and the resultant half steps, apart from the 7th chord built on the VII chord (B,D,F,A), the V7 chord is the only chord containing that powerful tritone interval, where each note of that interval is able to resolve a half step within the scale.[30] For this reason, the other non-dominant seventh chords generally do not have as strong a tendency to move to other chords. In place, the 7th note in these chords, with some exceptions, is often used more as coloring and shading, in some ways creating a pastel like quality of shade as opposed to the strong lines of the dominant chord. Now having noted this more passive role of the non-dominant diatonic 7th chords, we will also see that these chords, particularly in the world of jazz harmony (and in all idioms employing jazz harmony), can evolve with a bit of 'seasoning' into chords playing a more dominant role. Below we will examine one of the primary steps in that process.

---

30. In the key of C, the triadic VII chord contains the notes B-D-F and the resultant tritone. Notice these notes are the same notes as the 2nd, 3rd, and 4th note of the G7 chord. Due to this commonality, the diminished chord is often used functionally as a dominant type chord.

EXPANDING THE ROLE OF THE V7

The following idea is very simple yet provides the basis for much of what allows harmony to be expanded within and without the diatonic system. Here it is: every chord has a V7 chord that leads to it! Another way of saying this is that it is not just the I chord that has its associated V7 chord. Yes, within the diatonic system, the V7 chord defined within the scale (G7 in our example) is likely to be the most dominant of any V7 chord that may occur, but it may not be the only dominant chord used in a given song or composition.

Introducing this idea can easily lead to confusion due to the addition of yet even more numerical terms, some the same as others we have covered, yet meaning different things. On the plus side, this will give us another opportunity to increase our overall understating of the concepts illuminated by the terms. To explain further: within the context of a diatonic scale, the V7 chord is what it is: in our default example, it is the G7 that can lead to the home chord C. When we discuss the idea that each chord has its own V7 chord, we are talking about a different V7 chord. Here is an example. Let's take the IV chord in the C major diatonic scale system F-A-C. Using the principle that every chord has its own V7 chord, we only need to find the note an interval of a fifth above the F to determine the root note of the chord that will be the V7 to the F chord. This interval note is C. For the next step, we merely need to build a dominant chord on this root note C, which results in the chord C7.

Ex. 3-12

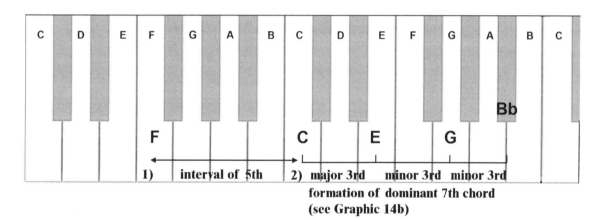

These 2 steps can be taken to determine the V7 chord of each chord within our diatonic system. The result is as follows: the V7 of D minor is A7, the V7 of E minor is B7, the V7 of F is C7, the V7 of G is D7, and the V7 of A minor is E7. We will look at these non-diatonic V7 chords more closely in the following section.

50   Western Harmony Simplified

Ex. 3-13

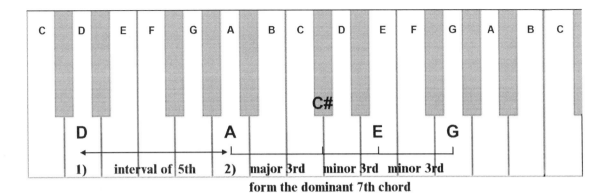

This might be a good place for all of us to take a breath, especially those who may be inundated with all the terms and somewhat technical information that has framed much of this discussion. This is also a good place to face this problem at its most basic level. Essentially, what is absolutely necessary and will hasten one's understanding of the harmonic system is becoming fluent with the intervals contained within the scale system. Over the course of time, the intervals can become second nature, but it's going to help this study if we can give this process another kick start. The intervals were laid out on page 40 and for your convenience in the Intervals Appendix. What I suggest here is for the reader to review this section and then take the time to apply the information to the keyboard. Become familiar with the way these intervals appear visually. In the C major scale, this only requires a limited amount of visual memorization, most of which is based on symmetric patterns (for example: the distance between C and G (an interval of a fifth) is the same as the distance between D and A (also an interval of a fifth). And – remember, to use your ears to become familiar with the sound of each of these intervals!

To make things even easier, think of this: seconds are easy to see, they are merely a note away from each other; thirds are two notes away from each other. Fourths and fifths are probably better understood by not necessarily counting notes or half steps in between, but by becoming familiar with the physical distance between the notes. As noted above, there is a definite symmetry, something similar to the way intervallic patterns on guitar repeat in the same shape. But be careful with this - when reviewing the intervals, please take into account that there are some exceptions to the perfect symmetry due to the asymmetrical placement of 2 black notes and 3 black notes within the 12 notes of the octave range. (Depending on placement within the scale, white notes one apart might be either major or minor seconds. Similarly, as was noted before, notes two apart could form an interval of either a major or minor third.)

Finally, with regard to learning the intervals, at this point, it is most important to become familiar with the intervals of fourths and fifths. As the I, IV, and V chords are the most common foundational chords within the diatonic system, it is essential that knowledge of these chords, whose root notes are separated by intervals of fourths and fifths, becomes second nature. This working knowledge will also be required in order to visualize the chord a fifth away from any chord in the system (any chord can have its own V7 chord as discussed above). Again, within our C major scale system, there are a limited number of possibilities; learning the intervals should therefore not be too great a task.[31]

> **31.** Additional tips for learning intervals: 1) visualize intervals at or away from the keyboard, 2) play the intervals and using the sense of touch feel the distance between, 3) as noted previously, find a song that starts with the interval and sing the notes.

BACK FROM INTERVAL LAND

To this point we have looked at the diatonic scale system and its chords. We have also seen we can form chords based on the diatonic scale either from 3 notes (triads) or 4 notes (7th chords). We also saw that the I, IV, and V chords are the most commonly used chords and discussed some of the reasons for their primacy. We noted that the V7 chord (the dominant) plays an important role as it provides a strong tension and release to the home chord (the I chord). We also expanded this idea noting that any chord can have a chord a fifth away functioning as a V7 chord. It is this latter idea where we will continue, stretching a little further, allowing us to expand our harmonic palette and gently enter the non-diatonic world.

CHAPTER IV: INTRODUCING NON-DIATONIC NOTES AND 2 NEW SCALES

Before we tackle the introduction of non-diatonic notes into our system, a reminder that the whole point of the system presented in this book is to simplify the world of Western harmony. Accordingly, here is the nutshell on the significance of non-diatonic notes and scales with respect to our diatonic system: Non-diatonic notes will be introduced for three reasons: 1) as we will see directly below, in order to form a dominant type chord that moves to a diatonic chord; 2) in order to form a dominant chord that will serve to move the harmony into a new key; and, 3) as we will see in a later chapter, to color diatonic chords with notes functioning to create tension and then release (a type of 'quasi' dominant), or simply to sustain tension.

Initially, we will introduce notes outside the diatonic scale in order to form a dominant chord that can move to a diatonic chord or in order to change key. For this analysis and to further the goal of simplicity, we will be introducing just two of the five available non-diatonic notes in the key of C, the notes F# and Bb.

The note F#, THE D7 CHORD AND THE G MAJOR SCALE

Remember, every chord has a chord that can serve as its dominant chord. The chord G, the V chord in the C major system has a chord that can function as its dominant V7 chord. This chord is D7 (the root note of the V7 (D7) chord (D) is an interval of a fifth away from the root note of the chord to which it will resolve – (G)). As we have seen, a V7 chord is formed with intervals of a major third, minor third, and minor third. Accordingly, the F# and C are the 3rd and 7th notes of the D7 chord. Just as the 3rd and 7th of the G7 chord resolve strongly to notes of the C chord, the F# and C of the D7 chord resolve strongly to the G and B of the G chord.

Ex. 4-1

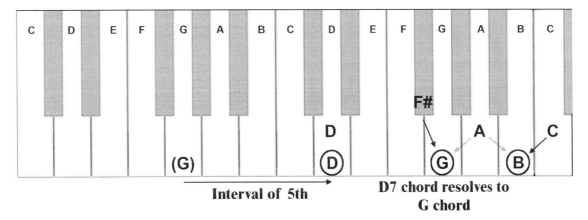

This is effectively why the F# non-diatonic note is required: in order to create that strong tension and release point between half-step neighbor notes. The D7 chord is built with the same intervallic relationship as the G7 chord. If you count the half steps in between, you will see that the F# is required as part of this structure. Also, notice if you play these chords on the piano, apart from sounding in a different register, you will hear a similarity in the type of chord – that is, the harmonic color evoked.

Introducing the F# allows us to enter a new key. Let's assume, as we have been, that we are writing or playing a song in the key of C. Suddenly, there appears a D7 chord (which incorporates the non-diatonic note F#). We can understand the use of this note from the above analysis – the D7 is serving as a dominant type chord simply to move to the G chord. This D7 chord, however, could be serving a more expansive purpose – to actually change keys, or as has been described, the 'home feeling' of the song, to the key of G. In some situations, it might be difficult (and perhaps not even important beyond the theoretical) to determine which of the two roles the D7 has served. Nevertheless, assuming the D7 chord did function in order to change keys, we would then enter the scale of G major which would become the new diatonic system. Just as we build the C major scale based on a step and half-step se-

Western Harmony Simplified

quential pattern, the G major scale (and all other scales) is built on this same pattern. Accordingly, the notes of this scale are G,A,B,C,D,E,**F#**,G.

Ex. 4-2

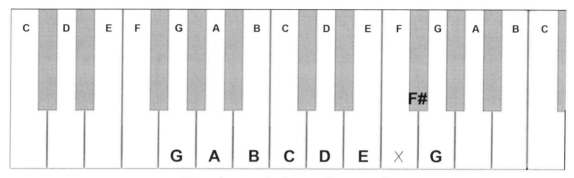

G major scale has only one sharp

All aspects of the system as we described for C major could then be applied to this G major diatonic scale system.

Review the G major scale - G,A,B,C,D,E,**F#**,G. Play this on the piano and/or study the example provided. Notice that this scale only has one black note, the F#. Memorize this sequence visually as well as in note name. Practice singing (out loud or to yourself) or whistling the notes of the scale. The sound should be the same as the C major scale, only starting on a different root note. Become familiar with its aural quality; this will hasten your learning of the major scales in other keys.

The note Bb, THE C7 CHORD AND THE F MAJOR SCALE

For the sake of practice and introducing a scale system incorporating flats, let's examine the V7 chord that moves to F, the IV chord in the key of C major. As noted above, every chord has a chord that can serve as its V7 dominant type chord. The chord with the root note an interval a fifth away from the root note F of F major is C. We then form a dominant chord with C as the root which is C7. Again, just as above, notice that the third and seventh note of the C7 chord (E and Bb) move magnetically towards the F and A notes of the F chord.

Ex. 4-3

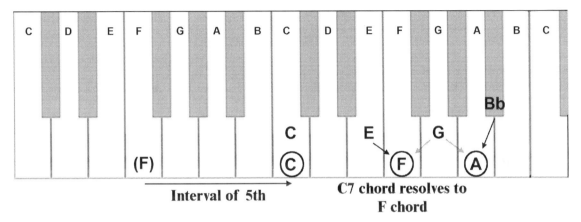

This C7 chord introduces the non-diatonic note (in relation to the C major scale) - Bb. As in the example above, this chord could simply be used as a vehicle to arrive to the IV chord (F) of C major.

The Bb note of the C7 chord can also be used as a means to arrive not only to the F chord, but to the F scale system – in other words, a key change. As above with the key change to G, this change may occur if the song or composition arrives to the F and stays there for a significant amount of time, making the key of F a temporary or permanent home. The F scale would then become the new diatonic material from which to build chords and derive melody. This scale is: F,G,A,**Bb**,C,D,E,(F). Again, notice this scale is structured in the exact sequential step and half-step pattern as the C major and G major scales. Review this new scale: F,G,A,**Bb**,C,D,E,(F).

Ex. 4-4

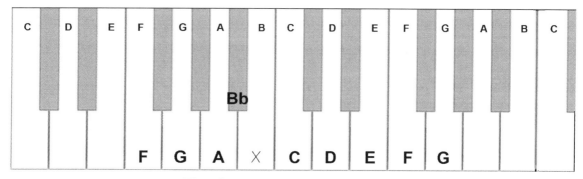

F major scale has only one flat

Again, notice there is only one black note in this scale. The memorization of this scale, in addition to the C major (all white notes) and the G major scales, should be a painless task. Use visual recognition to develop a familiarity.

Reviewing the Seventh Chord

Before moving to the next section where fluency with 7th chords will be required, a little housekeeping is in order. What follows is yet another review and caution about terms and numerical identifiers. It is necessary and will help simplify the analysis moving forward. Please take the time for this review before moving on.

Thus far, we have identified the following 7th chord types within the diatonic system. C major 7 (also F major 7), D minor 7 (also E minor 7 and A minor 7) and G7. [32]

> **32.** Within the C major diatonic system there is also E minor 7, F major 7, and A minor 7. These minor chords are structured exactly as the D minor 7 chord as the F major 7 chord is structured exactly as the C major 7.

58   Western Harmony Simplified

Ex. 4-5

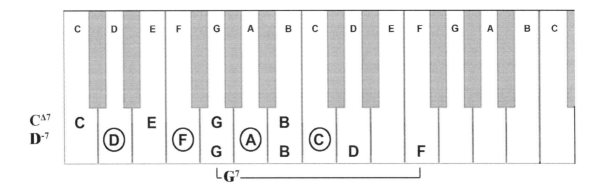

What is crucial to understand and to be able to differentiate is exactly what the major, minor, and 7 monikers are identifying. Let's take the first chord, C major 7. Remember that a C chord does not need to be identified as a major chord. When no name is given to a chord, other than the letter name, we can assume it is a major chord. Therefore, the major 7 part of the C major 7 moniker is referring to the *type of 7th interval* relative to the root note C. As we have examined before, a major 7 interval is 11 half steps or – easier, you can find the major 7 interval by locating the note one half step below the octave above the root.

Ex. 4-6

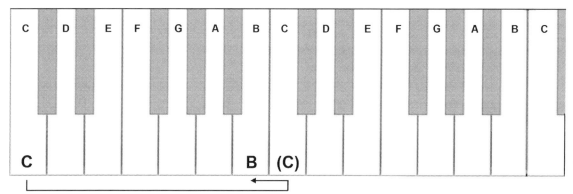

The major 7 interval is 1/2 step
below the octave above the root

Got it? From now on, in order to identify the C (major 7) or any other (major 7) chord, the △ will be used as shorthand for major – the result for the diatonic C chord will be **C△7**.[33] Remember that △7 chords have a particular sound. Play it at the piano and listen to the quality of the harmony.

33. Some will identify this chord as C maj7; my preference is for the simpler triangle symbol.

Now, taking the D minor 7 — As minor chords do need to be identified, the minor moniker of D minor 7 is referring to the *chord type.* The 7 of the D minor 7 is identifying the type of seventh that is being used. Here, this is a rule you must digest before moving on. When a chord is identified as a 7 chord (not a △7), the interval is a distance 10 half steps above the root or a step below the octave above the root note.

Ex. 4-7

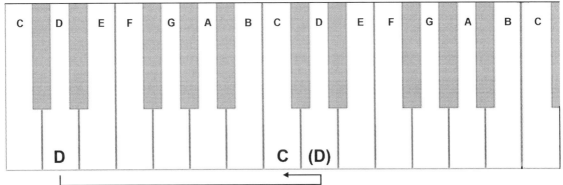

The minor 7 interval is a whole step
below the octave above the root

It would be worthwhile here if you have access to a piano (or alternatively use the example provided) to play through the seventh chords that comprise the C major diatonic system: C△7, D-7, E-7, F△7, G7, A-7 and B°7. Notice that the 7th interval in the major 7 chords is different than the 7th interval of the 7 chords. Please also take note, D minor 7 can alternatively be written as Dm7 or Dmin7, or D-7 in place of D minor 7. Here and forward I will be using the simple symbol - to identify the chord as minor.[34]

> **34.** What notes are contained in the chord A-△7? The A- is referencing the A minor chord (notes A, C, and E) and the △7 is referencing the type of seventh being used in the chord. Since a major 7 interval is found by moving down one half step from the octave above the root, the resulting note here is G#. The A-△7 therefore consists of the notes A, C, E, and G#.

Western Harmony Simplified

CHAPTER V: EXPANSION

The II V I Sequence - Common Patterns in Harmony

We have already discussed how the I, IV and V chords are the essential building blocks of Western harmony. It was also noted that whole genres of music might be built on these simple triadic chords, with little or no use of other chords within the diatonic system. At the same time, there are as many genres of music that incorporate not only other diatonic chords, but use a chord's dominant chord to arrive to the chords (as we discussed in the previous section with D7 moving to G and C7 moving to F). These same styles often utilize certain sequences of chords that become more and more recognizable with experience. Understanding a few of these patterns and learning to hear them will give you a head start on this process of recognition. This will also be extremely useful in learning new songs because songs are often built on these recognizable chord sequences.

One of the most common sequences of chords (also commonly known as chord "progressions") found in various genres of music is what is referred to as the II V I. In the key of C, the II V I progression consists of the chords D minor to G to C. (Remember that the diatonic II chord in the C major scale system is D minor, the V is G, and the I chord is C. This sequence is fully diatonic as there are no notes outside the key of C used within any of these chords.) Within many styles of music, some or all of the chords of this D minor to G to C pattern are expanded beyond simple triads into 4 note 7th chords. The resulting chords are D-7 to G7 to C (or C△7). Notice that this sequence is still fully diatonic.[35]

> **35.** <u>Another important bit of housekeeping</u> – Roman numeral references to the II chord, V chord, or for that matter any of the diatonic chords are contextual. That is, a chord written as a II chord in many contexts may actually be referring to a II minor or II minor 7 chord, just as a "V" chord is in many
>
> (continued)

instances referring to a V7 chord. This is generally done for shorthand so please don't be confused by this seeming inconsistency. In a later lesson, we will see that the II chord can be turned into a dominant chord (with a similar structure to the V7 chord). This chord will be identified as a II7 chord.

Ex. 5-1

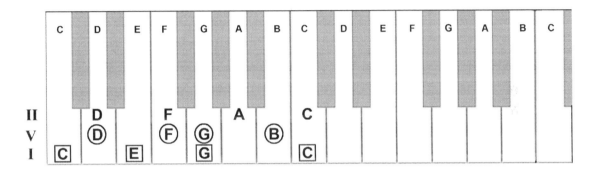

If you have access to a keyboard, play the above sequence of chords and get a sense of its sound and structure. You might notice that the D-7 chord is very close to the IV (F) chord as the former contains all of the latter's notes F, A, and C. We can see therefore that the II V I sequence is very close to the IV V I sequence that is also prevalent through various musical styles.[36]

36. With more study and hands on experience, you will find that there are many examples of this interchangeability of the chords in the diatonic system. Other examples of chords sharing common notes are the chords C and E- sharing the notes E and G, and the chords C and A- sharing the notes C and E. The chords F and D-, as well as C and E-, are often used interchangeably in the jazz idiom.

(continued)

Ex. 5-2

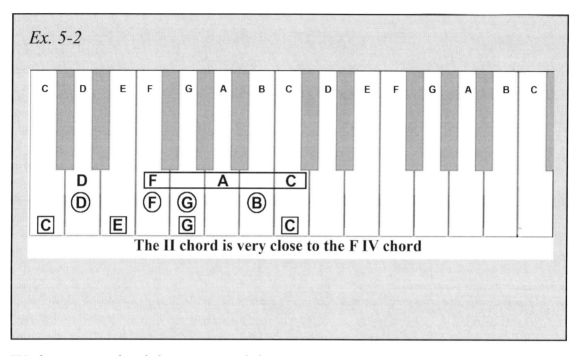

The II chord is very close to the F IV chord

We have examined the II V I and the IV V I in the key of C as two examples of common progressions. Now, building on the idea that any chord can have its own V chord (we looked at the C7 moving to F and the D7 moving to G as two examples), each chord within a diatonic system can also have its own II V sequence leading to it. Another way to understand this is that, yes, any chord within the system can have a V chord that leads to it, but also, any of these 'V' chords can then be 'modified' into a II V sequence. Accordingly, within our C major diatonic system, two common sequences emerge (as well as others covered later). One is the G-7 to C7 leading to the F (modifying the V7 to F (C7) into a II V). The other is the B-7 b5 to E7 leading to A- (modifying the V7 (E7) into a II V).[37] What's important and practical about these progressions is that, in the process of learning songs, which is an extremely useful method of learning harmony, being aware of these patterns will significantly help to simplify and speed up this process. The more one looks at songs, the more the patterns will become distinguishable. Again, two of the most common patterns are the II V I to the IV chord of C (G-7 to C7 to F) and the II V I to the VI chord of C (B-7 b5 to E7 to A-).[38]

37. The use here of the terminology II V I to describe different chord sequences is another example of numbers being descriptive and related to context rather than being exclusive to particular chords within the diatonic system. YES, the primary II V I in the key of C is D-7 to G7 to C△7, but, as noted above, other chords within the same diatonic system can have their own II V sequences. The F is the IV chord of the C major diatonic system, but within the context of a preceding II V sequence, the F chord can function as a I chord with respect to the II V (G-7 C7) chords.

38. We have yet to address the minor scale which contains the minor 7 b5 chord as one of its diatonic chords. We will look at the minor scale system in short time. Fortunately, it is largely based on the major scale we have already studied. The II Vs to a minor chord will then easily fall into place.

Ex. 5-3

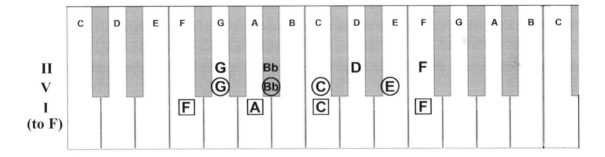

Ex. 5-4

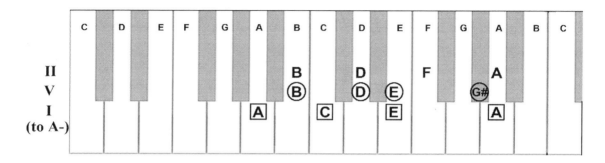

THE II V I - - IMPLICATIONS AND EXTRAPOLATIONS
(The V of the V)

The D-7 G7 C (△7 optional) sequence appears at first glance to contain one V chord in addition to the II chord and the I chord. A more advanced and useful way to see the D-7 II chord, however, is to understand that it is also functioning as a sort of V chord to the G7. (Remember, every chord has a chord that can serve as its V7 chord or quasi-dominant chord.) Notice the note C of the II chord (D-7) resolves to the note B of the G chord.

Ex. 5-5

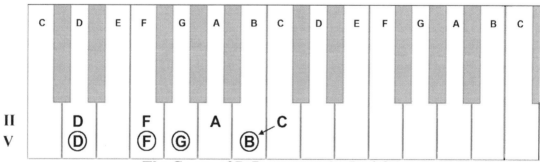

The C note of D-7 moves to the B of G7

This is similar to the F note of the G7 chord resolving a half step down to the E note of the C chord when playing a V7 -> I progression in the key of C (remember the power of the tension and release of the notes a half step apart). In sum, the D-7 to G7 to C progression can be looked at this way: D-7 is serving as a type of V chord to the G7 which is serving as a V chord to C, the I chord. Notice that the D root of the D-7 chord is an interval of a fifth above the G root of the G7 chord – just as the G root of the G7 chord is a fifth above the C root of the C chord.

You may have noticed that even as I laid out the dominant type role played by D-7 moving to G, there is a clear difference between this D-7 as it moves to G and the G7 as it moves to C. That is: the G7 contains a major third (G to **B**) as the second note of the chord while the D-7 contains a minor third (D to **F**) as the second note. This is an important distinction for reasons addressed earlier. The G7 chord GBDF has two points of tension and release as it moves to the C chord: the F note of the G chord resolves to the E of the C chord AND the B note of the G chord resolves to the C of the C chord.

Ex. 5-6

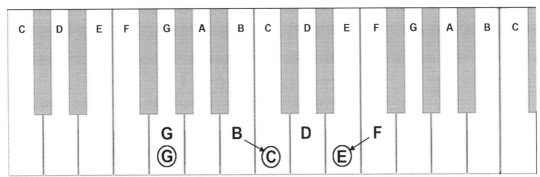

The B and D of G7 move to C and E of the C chord

This double pronged tension and release is what gives this chord sequence its inherent power. In the D-7 to G7 sequence, while there's not as much power in the release, the C note of the D-7 chord still does release to the B of the G7 chord - enough to create the inherent pull of a dominant to tonic

Western Harmony Simplified 67

relationship. We will see below that there is a quick and easy way to maximize this attraction.

DISCRETIONARY DOMINANT CHORDS

Theory is made to come alive by the composers and instrumentalists of the music world. In fact, there remains the question whether composers and instrumentalists preceded the theory or whether the theory is just being discovered. In any event, the way in which composers and instrumentalists have dealt with the II-7 chord (in our examples D-7) may shed some light on this question if not quite answering it definitively.

Notably in the area of jazz, r&b, blues, and pop where improvisation and composition are closely linked, the II-7 chord is often turned into a full dominant chord at the discretion of the player or composer (replacing the minor third with a major third).

Ex. 5-7

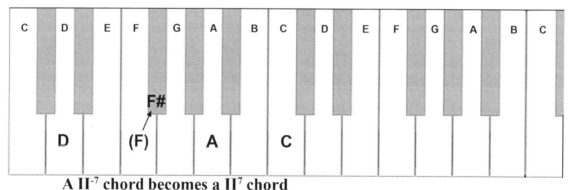

A II^{-7} chord becomes a II^7 chord
by using a major third instead of a minor third

This discretion is used in order to shape harmonic color which is so malleable in the jazz influenced idioms. These idioms are deeply connected to the soul/blues 'feel,' a feel sometimes better expressed with a well placed dominant chord rather than a minor 7 chord. Remember in the initial introduction to 7th chords, listening to the quality and distinctive colors of each of the chords – the dominant 7, minor 7, and major 7. Listen again within the context of the II V I sequence; turn the II-7 into a II7 chord (D-7 becomes D7) and notice the difference.[39] This discretion will be examined in more depth when we look at the harmonic structure of blues where dominant chords play a more (for lack of a better term) *dominant* role. In any event, these examples further illustrate that the II chord can serve a dominant type role, in effect being a dominant to a dominant (V7 to V7 chord).

> **39.** Two examples of the dominant being used in the II chord are in Duke Ellington's "Take the A Train" and "Mood Indigo" where in both, the I chords are followed by the dominant II.

MORE ON THE V7 TO V7 CHORD, DISCRETIONARY CHORDS AND THE POWER OF THE 3RD AND 7th NOTE OF THE CHORD

In addition to the discretion to turn the II-7 into a dominant chord (II7), there is also discretion to turn the III and VI chords which are diatonically minor chords into dominant chords (E-7 becomes E7 and A-7 becomes A7).[40]

> **40.** Welcome to two new black notes the G# and C#! These notes are part of the E7 and A7 chords. These two chords are formed in the same way as the dominant seventh chords we have already covered, the G7 and D7.

Western Harmony Simplified

Ex. 5-8

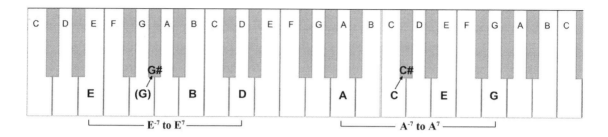

Again, this choice tends to color the music as distinctively 'bluesy.' This type of chording is used not only in the blues style; it is widely employed in jazz, pop, salsa, Brazilian, and R&B and soul. Here, we have another instance of a V type chord moving to a V chord. The analysis is the same as what we saw in a discretionary D7 moving to G7, which revealed a V type chord moving to a V chord. In the movement from a III chord to a VI chord, if the III and VI chords are turned into dominants (E7 and A7 instead of E-7 and A-7) there is essentially a movement from a V7 to V7 chord. Taking this a step further, in the common progression, III VI II V, it is possible that there will be in effect movement from a V to a V to a V to a V to a I chord! (E7 to A7 to D7 to G7 to C). The E chord is a 5th above the A chord which is a 5th above the D chord which is a 5th above the G chord which is a 5th above C. The first 4 chords are dominant and lead strongly to the next by way of the pull of the 3rd and 7th notes (remember how these notes are a half step away from notes in the chord of resolution). The illustration following outlines this movement.

Ex. 5-9

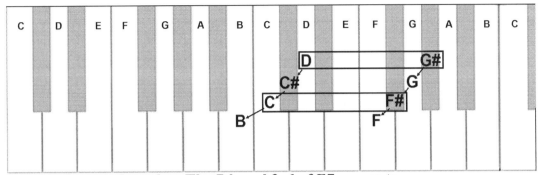

In order: The 7th and 3rd of E7 moves to the 3rd and 7th of the A7 (C# and G) which moves to the 7th and 3rd of D7 (C and F#) which moves to the 3rd and 7th of G7 (B and F)

Once again, the power of the 3 and 7 of the scale (and chord) becomes clear. In the case of the discretionary dominant chord III7 (E7) moving to the discretionary dominant VI7 (A7), there are two points of half step voice leading creating a strong magnetic pull. From the E7 chord, the G# and D lead to the G and C# of the A7 chord. What is curious is that the G# D to G C# movement (a chromatic symmetrical movement down a half step) results in a 3 and 7 chord turning into a 7 and 3 chord.

Ex. 5-10

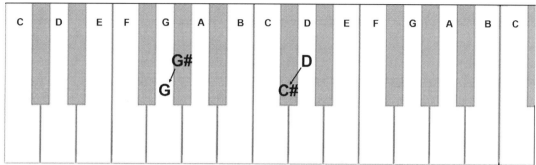

**G# and D, the 3rd and 7th of the E7 chord
resolves a half step down to the G and C#
(the 7th and the 3rd) of the A7 chord**

This is significant beyond the numeric curiosity. First, this allows for the chromatic pull that leads one V chord to the chord a 5th below as in E7 to A7 and/or D7 to G7 to C. We have already seen the strong pull of the V chord moving to a I chord or in this case another V chord. The 3 7 to 7 3 voice movement further enhances this attraction.

The 3 7 and 7 3 notes of the seventh chords have another important role and function. If one listens to a chord carefully to determine which notes most define that chord, the 3rd and 7th stand out. Clearly the 1st note is initially the most defining note as it allows us to know the root home base of the chord. However, if one plays the 1st and 5th note of the chord there is no way to tell anything about the character of the chord. Conversely, the 3rd and 7th note do just that; they tell us what kind of chord it will be – major or minor by way of the 3rd – and what kind of 7th chord it will be by way of the 7th note being a regular 7 or a major 7. The dominant chord is particularly recognizable in the 3 7 or 7 3 configuration even without any other indication of the root.[41] The dissonant tritone interval of this voicing leads the ear naturally to resolve the notes; the ear is accordingly likely to

41. Jazz players will often leave out the root and or 5th of the chord and the chord will still be recognizable.

72   Western Harmony Simplified

fill in the root note. In any event, this voicing is vital to the jazz and pop player as it defines chords and shows up within other more complex voicings (voicings containing the 3rd and 7th but also other notes). In addition to the player and composer understanding the diatonic scale system and the chords contained within, it is also important for musicians to develop a facility with common voicings. The 3 7 or 7 3 are two of these voicings.[42] Please see Appendix 9 - Standard Jazz Voicings - for further study and review.

> **42.** The 3 7 and 7 3 voicings indicate chords other than the dominant. The 3 7 or 7 3 can be a part of a X-7 or X△7 or X-△7. (Can you figure out what this last chord would be starting with A as X? This chord will be covered in detail on the section on the diatonic minor scale and chord system.) Answer: A-△7 includes the notes A C E and G#.

TRITONE SUBSTITUTION CHORDS

There is one other important connection to be made between the 3 7 and 7 3 chord voicings. This involves a somewhat advanced concept (yet simple at its basis) - the tritone substitution. This concept is based on the 3 7 inversion (voicing) reversing itself to 7 3 as it moves chromatically down a step to the chord a 5th below.

Ex. 5-11

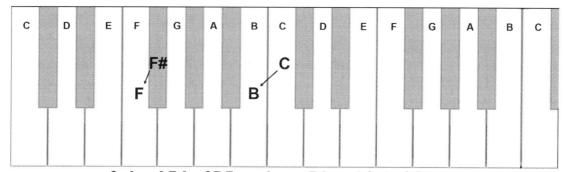

3rd and 7th of D7 resolve to 7th and 3rd of G7

With the tritone substitution, the change from 3 7 to 7 3 (or 7 3 to 3 7) occurs not by moving the chord, but by simply moving the bass note a tritone away from the root of the first chord. If we look at G7 for example and take the 3rd and 7th of that chord (B and F) and then move the bass note from G to Db, the B and F notes become the 7th and 3rd of the now Db7 chord. (consisting of Db F and Cb(B) – remember the 5th is not necessary to identify this chord). Assuming that this G7 was moving in sequence to the C chord (V to I), the Db7 moving to the C chord serves as a substitute dominant chord for G as it moves to the C chord. This concept can be applied to any chord or chord sequence. Play the sequence on a keyboard and notice the similarity of sound and functions between these two chords.

Ex. 5-12[43]

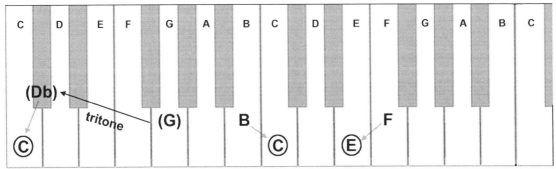

3rd and 7th of G⁷ become
the 7th and 3rd of Db⁷ which can
resolve to the C chord

> **43.** There are new black notes introduced in this example, the Db and Ab. For now, as we did when introducing the E7 and A7 chord, just understand that this Db dominant seventh chord (and other future examples of dominant seventh chords) is built with the same intervals as chords we have already examined.

For another example of this substitution concept as well as a bit of a review, let's assume that we are going to move from D7 to G7 and then to C. This is a discretionary dominant chord (the II-7 is turned into II7) moving to the V, which then moves to the I. The D7 is in effect serving as the V to the V chord (G7), which is moving to the I chord (C). Here's how the tritone substitution can work in this example: instead of moving directly from the D7 to the G7, we are going to move through the tritone substitution chords. The result will be D7 to ***Ab7*** (tritone substitution for D7) to G7 to ***Db7*** (tritone substitution for G7) and then to C. Looking at what is happening within the chords: the 3rd and 7th of the D7 (F# and C) stay in place while the bass note

Western Harmony Simplified

moves a tritone from D to Ab. The notes F# and C, originally the 3rd and 7th of the D7 chord then become the 7th and 3rd of the Ab7 chord.[44]

> **44.** Technically, the F# becomes a Gb when it is part of the Ab chord. Generally, when defining chords a mix of sharps and flats is not preferred.

Ex. 5-13

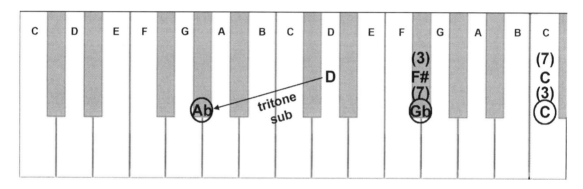

On the next step of the progression, the 7 3 of the Ab7 moves chromatically down a half step to the the F and B (7 3) of the G7 chord. This 7 3 of the G7 chord then becomes the 3 7 of the Db7 chord before finally completing the progression to C△7.

Ex. 5-14

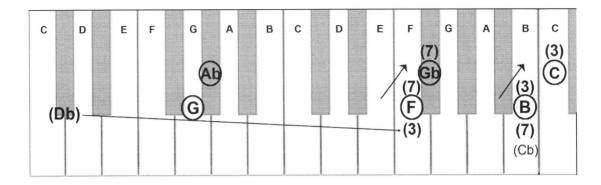

This harmonic behavior clearly shows the interchangeability of the tritone substitution dominant chord with the original dominant chord. This substitution is not only supported by theory, but works very well in practice and sound.

Another important lesson to be drawn from the tritone substitution chord is the additional example of the tension release effect of notes a half step apart. In the above paragraphs we have seen how the interchangeable 3 7 notes between the dominant and tritone substitute dominant chords resolve to notes a half step away in the destination chord (for example the F and B (or Cb) in the G7 or Db7 chord move to E and C of the C chord). There is also movement of the root note Db of the Db7 chord moving to the root note C. This movement is very strong as there is a lot of weight from not only a note a half step above, but from the root of a whole chord that is a half step above. While on the subject of the tendency or pull created by half step relationships - this attraction can be very strong if the chord above is the same as the chord below it. If, for example, the destination chord is a C△7, a Db△7 above will want to resolve to that C△7. Why? - because every note in the Db△7 chord is symmetrically a half step above the chord below. Turbo resolution! This is a widely used technique in jazz related idioms and can be used with various types of chords.

Ex. 5-15

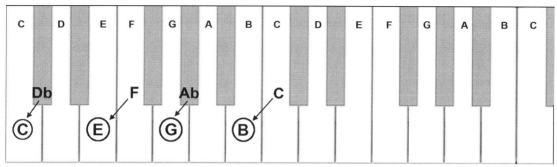

Db$^{\Delta 7}$ resolves to C$^{\Delta 7}$ in half steps

And finally, another important note before moving on: the attraction of the half steps, which we have visited now in various contexts, will surface again when this study moves into an examination of the upper structures of chords (9ths, 11ths, 13ths, b9s, #11s, etc.). Half-step movement functioning as a quasi-dominant to quasi root sequence will be a major part of the analysis as we look at the coloring of chords and the resolving voice movement within chords, an essential aspect of harmony that permeates many styles of music.

CHAPTER VI: THE SUSPENDED CHORD

THE "SUS" CHORD

Up to this point, we have examined the diatonic chords within C major including three types of seventh chords: the major seven, the minor seven, and the dominant seven. The 'sus' chord is a new entry to our palette and it significantly adds to the colors available in the diatonic template. It is structured using elements of chords we have already examined and functions as both a transitional chord and a chord with its own independent harmonic flavor.

In the classical tradition, composers commonly employed a 'raised third' note which had the effect of sustaining (or "suspending") tension within a chord. In the Key of C, an example of this sus chord would be playing the chord G-**C**-D followed by G-**B**-D (the V chord), then followed by G-C-E (the I chord in the 2nd position)[45]. The C note in the first chord (G **C** D) is the sustained note replacing the third note B of that chord. This 'suspended' C moves a half step down to the note B of the second chord G (a half step release) and then back up a half step to C of the final chord C.

> **45.** The notes ordered as CEG form the *root* position of the C chord, EGC the *first* position, and GCE the *second* position.

Western Harmony Simplified

Ex. 6-1

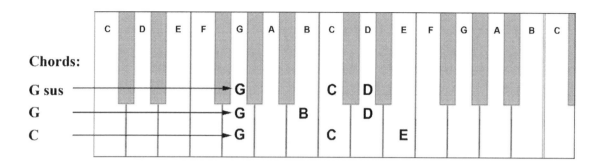

This 'sus' note in classical music was used primarily as a means of movement between chords. In the popular and jazz traditions, the sus chord - a chord with the 3rd raised a half step - is commonly used as a chord color that does not require resolution. The structure and application of these chords will be examined here.

The sus chord can be formed and identified in various ways. The example above, G-C-D, can be simply called a **G sus** chord (from G *suspended*). This is the most basic of the sus chords; it contains three notes: the root, suspended third (the fourth), and the fifth. The G sus chord can also be identified as a **Gsus7, F/G, D-7/G,** or **F△7/G**. The Gsus7 contains the notes G-C-D-F. The other sus chord types are **F/G,** which is an F chord (F-A-C) 'over' G in the bass; **D-7/G,** which is a D-7 (D-F-A-C) over G in the bass; and, **F△7/G,** which is an F△7 (F-A-C-E) over G in the bass. (The note to the right of the slash is the single bass note, to the left, the chord).

Ex. 6-2

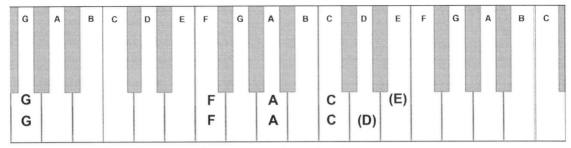

Various types of sus chords

Within jazz and its related idioms, a sus chord generally will contain more notes than the G-C-D sus chord, utilizing one of (or something similar to) the chords listed above: Gsus7, F/G, D-7/G, or F△7/G. Rock and some pop tunes less inflected with jazz harmony tend to use the simple form of the sus chord (G-C-D). This latter chord has a particular sound to it; a good example of this is the keyboard figure on the verse of the Who's "Pinball Wizard." This sound is very different from the sus chord used in jazz related idioms so it is important to have the chord properly identified. Having said this, in my own musical travels, I have mostly used the moniker "sus" chord as a reference to one of the more complex sus chords (i.e., F△7/G). Because I am often working in jazz influenced idioms, I expect the players to understand the context and not play the simple form of the sus chord.

This 'jazz' type sus chord has a unique feature that creates more opportunity for the discretion of the player or composer. <u>Essentially, this sus chord is a II V progression built into one chord.</u> The most clear example of this is the sus chord identified as D-7/G. Here, we can see that in the Key of C, the sus chord is the II-7 over the bass note G, the G which happens to be root of the V chord. So, in effect, the sus chord can be seen as a II-7/V, a combination of the II and V chords.

Western Harmony Simplified

Ex. 6-3

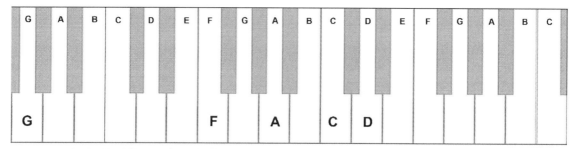

D-7 is the II chord in C; the notes G, F, and D form part of the V chord in C

Looking at the notes of this chord sheds light in another way – not only is there the D-7 contained in this chord G-*D-F-A-C*, but there is something very close to a G7 chord with only a C replacing the 3rd note B of the G7 *G-D-F*-A-*C*.[46] Remember that the note C is the sustained note, the one in the classical world that would likely resolve to B. In our modern usage of the sus chord, the sustained note may or may not resolve to the third. In either case, if the sustained note C does resolve to B, the G sus chord becomes a G7, and the II V sequence will have effectively played itself out. If the sus note is not resolved, there is enough of both chords (the D-7 and G7) within this one sus chord to give the ear a sense of having progressed through the two chords. If you play D-7/G and then move to a C chord, you can hear this progression and at least a somewhat satisfying resolution.

> **46.** The A note is diatonic but is considered an extension of the chord – a 9th. We will be looking at these 'upper structure' notes of chords at length in a later chapter.

As we saw above, there are clearly two chords, the II and the V contained in the sus chord D-7/G. You might then ask - what about the other types of sus chords described above, the Gsus7, F/G, and F△7/G? Does the above analy-

82   Western Harmony Simplified

sis apply? The simple answer is yes, there are enough common notes within each of these chords to produce the same effect. Specifically, each of the above chords contains the notes F and C which happen to be our old friend the 3rd and 7th of the D-7 chord. We saw in an earlier chapter the importance and defining aspect of the 3rd and 7th of a chord. Within the sus chord, this 3rd and 7th (in relation to D-7) provide enough of the quality of that chord to prove the point – all sus chords in effect contain a II chord and a V chord.

Ex. 6-4

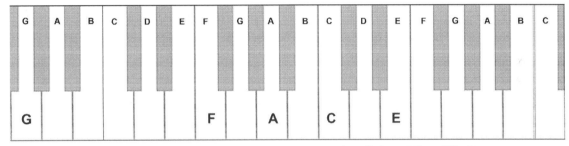

The F and C of this chord can be seen as the 3rd and 7th of D-7

This interchangeability of the sus chords recalls an earlier point. In my musical dealings, I refer simply to the sus chord as a sus chord and rarely define it as I did above (Gsus7, F/G, and F△7/G). As these chords produce the same effect, which sus chord gets used is often left to the discretion of the player.

> **47.** The song "Black Cow" is one example among many.

There may be situations where the exact chord will be required; as I mentioned before, the use of the sus in rock is often quite specific. The F/G chord also has its own 'vibe,' one only needs to listen to Steely Dan to get a good dose of this chord's pleasurable lean richness.[47]

THE SUS CHORD AND DISCRETION

As another example of the many available harmonic choices around the II V sequence, we also have the option to turn any V7 dominant chord into a sus chord. In practice, the player/composer has the discretion to turn any V7 chord into a II V sequence. This V7 chord can be the V7 of the root chord of a diatonic system (i.e., G7 to C which would become a D-7 to G7 to C), or a dominant chord serving as a V7 to another chord within the diatonic system (i.e., C7 to F becoming G-7 to C7 to F). Following this further, since the sus chord's structure contains both a II and a V, it is a logical step that there is discretion to replace any V dominant chord with a sus chord as a 'substitute' for the II V sequence. The inverse of this is true as well. If a musician encounters a sus chord, it is possible to play this chord as a two chord sequence. (For example: Gsus7 can be played as D-7 to G.)

This discretion goes even further in the world of improvised jazz. A somewhat simple option is to choose to play a V7 chord in place of an indicated II V sequence. Similarly, the music may indicate a sus chord and here again, a musician could choose to move directly to the V7 chord. These choices are made on the basis of the mood of the music at the time and whether the player wants to employ a sus chord for its rich color, move directly to a dominant chord to evoke that sound, or to play a II V sequence to move the harmonic rhythm through two chords instead of one.

The available harmonic options in jazz with respect to the V7 chord can get more and more complex. We looked previously at the tritone substitution option as applied to a V7 chord (Db7 instead of G7). This substitution when applied to the sus chord can lead to some interesting configurations. If you think of the various harmonic choices discussed through these chapters around the V7: the II V, the V7 only, a sus chord, making the II of the II V sequence a dominant chord instead of a minor 7, and then apply all these possibilities to the tritone substitution chord, the possibilities are great. For example, let's say that a song presents a D-7 to G7 resolving to a C△7. Some of the possible ways to play this sequence are: D-7 to Gsus to C△7, D7 to G7 to C△7,[48] D-7 to Ab7 to G7 to C△7,[49] D7 to Ab7 to Gsus7 to Db7 to C△7,[50] D-7 to Ab7 to Gsus7

> **48.** Discretion to turn II-7 chord into a dominant which becomes a V of the V.

to Dbsus7 to C△7,[51] D-7 to Eb-7 to Ab7 to G7 to Ab-7 to Dbsus7 to C△7.[52] You get the picture? The possibilities are great and these varied choices are part of what allows jazz to be such a rich and exciting improvisational idiom. Within a group of players, hearing and coordinating these chord choices can be worked out beforehand or left for the spontaneity of the moment. The tempo, arrangement and general feeling of the music will help to give a logical context to these choices. In most settings, the goal is not to play the most complex available chord sequence, rather, it is to play the most musical.

Before moving into the diatonic system on the other side of the tracks - the minor scale and its related chords - one other point should be made concerning the discretionary chords that keep emerging in this discussion. If any of you have tried to play through these sequences, and in particular tried to apply some of the substitutions and discretionary chords, you may have found that the sequences may not sound inspired. There could be a few reasons for this. First, it will take some practice and experience in voicing chords to move through these sequences in a way that is satisfying to the ear. Please visit appendices (2 and 4) to access exercises designed to help in this area; the importance of learning proper voicing and voice leading cannot be overstressed. Second, in a later

---

49. Ab7 is a tritone substitution for a discretionary D7. The sequence could have been D-7 to D7.

50. Ab7: tritone substitution; Gsus7: any dominant chord can be turned into a sus chord.

51. Dbsus7: started as a tritone substitution for G7, turned into a sus because any dominant chord can be turned into a sus chord.

52. Eb-7 to Ab7 derived from the tritone substitution Ab7 which was derived from the discretionary dominant D7 which replaced the II-7 (D-7); simply, any dominant can be turned into a sus chord or a II V.

Western Harmony Simplified

chapter we will look at the possible notes that can be played in addition to the 4 notes of the basic seven chord. These are notes sometimes referred to as extensions, tensions, or upper structure notes (yes, yet even more discretion![53]), and will help to provide the coloring and connecting points between chords.

> **53.** Don't worry, we are almost at the end of laying out the forest.

CHAPTER VII: THE MINOR DIATONIC SYSTEM

Until here, we have looked at the C major diatonic system. We are now going to look at the minor scale system which fortunately is built in large part from the same notes and chords as the major diatonic system. The connection between the systems is this – every major scale system has a *relative minor* scale system which starts three half steps (an interval of a minor third) below the first note of the major scale and uses the same notes as that *relative* major scale. In C major, the note three half steps below C is A; A is the first note and root of the A minor scale system. The commonality of tones between the C major and A minor scales means once fluency has been developed in the major scale, fluency in the relative minor scale is only a few steps away.

THE THREE MINOR SCALES

While the A minor scale is built on the notes of the C major scale, it is also a bit more complex than its relative major; for example, in certain instances, the A minor scale uses two notes outside of the C scale, F# and G# (the 6th and 7th degree of the A minor scale). These notes are not used all the time, for example, the scale may be purely diatonic (in relation C to major) using A,B,C,D,E,F,G and A. This latter scale using only the note material contained in C major (all white notes!) is called the A "**natural minor**" scale. There are two other scales that can be used for the minor key. These scales move outside of a pure diatonic relationship with C major by way of the notes F and G. The first of these scales is A "**harmonic minor**" which incorporates the notes A,B,C,D,E,*F and G#*. The second of these scales is the A "**melodic minor**" and moves ascending with the notes A,B,C,D,E,*F#, G#* and A and descending by way of the notes A,*G,F*,E,D,C,B, and A.

Ex. 7-1

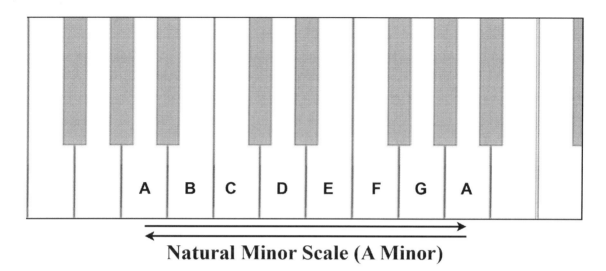

Natural Minor Scale (A Minor)

Ex. 7-2

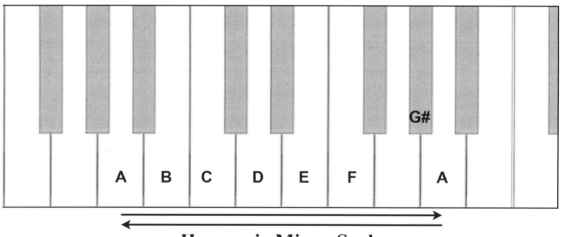

Harmonic Minor Scale

Ex. 7-3

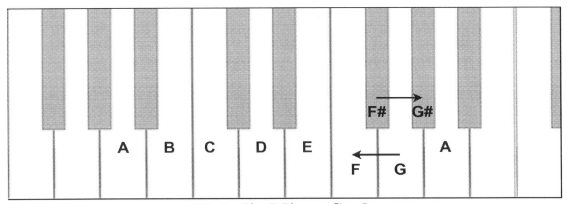

Melodic Minor Scale

There are a few reasons for the use of the three scales in the minor key - the natural minor, the harmonic minor, and the melodic minor. We already saw that the natural minor is simply the pure diatonic relative minor of the C scale (it uses only the notes from the C scale). The harmonic minor scale's use of the G# is explained by a phenomenon that we have already examined in depth – the power of the V7 chord to the I chord. Remember - the dominant chord is built on the root, the major third above (four half steps), followed by a minor third and another minor third (each three half steps). As you can see, this V7 in the key of A starting with E contains the notes E *G#* B and D.

Ex. 7-4

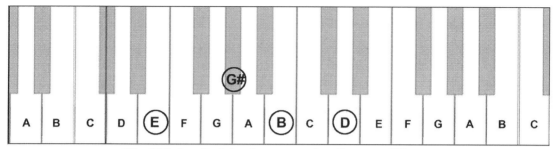

The V7 chord of A minor contains the note G#

If we used only the pure diatonic notes of A natural minor, the V chord would be E-7 and would not have the resolving power inherent in that G# half step relation to A. So simply, the G# is used to allow the V chord in the key of A minor to be a true dominant chord. This G# is also known as a leading tone for its natural character in the scale to lead melodically to the A.

Another point regarding the harmonic minor scale: while we can clearly see the chord related purpose for the use of the G#, we should also notice that the resultant scale turns out to have, if not an oriental sound, at least something evocative of Eastern Europe. This scale has been and continues to be used by composers and improvisers in a variety of contexts and is certainly useful beyond its purpose of building a dominant V chord.

The melodic minor scale presents other challenges for understanding the minor diatonic system. At the same time, this scale indicates the flexibility and discretion that permeates the minor system allowing for various creative choices in composition and performance. To review, the melodic minor scale ascends by way of the notes A,B,C,D,E,F#, G# and A and descends by way of A,G,F,E,D,C,B, and A. Again, we can see that the difference in this scale is the treatment of the 6th and 7th degree. It makes sense based on our analysis of the harmonic minor scale that the G# is incorporated to allow the V7 (E7) chord to be a dominant chord leading strongly to the I (A minor) home/tonic chord. In the ascending scale, the G# is followed by the A; this is the powerful half step movement to A both in the scale and within the E7 chord as it resolves to A minor. Going down the scale, the G# does not serve any purpose of resolution to the F, so we can see it is not necessary to incorporate it as part of the descending scale.

The Harvard Dictionary of Music offers a different raison d'etre for the melodic minor scale's variance on the 6th and 7th degrees. It notes that if the scale were to descend from A by way of the G# and F#, the scale would sound too much like a major scale. (The C major scale descends from C with a half step to B and then a whole step to A. Descending from A to G# to F# is exactly this same sequence of intervals contained in the C major scale and is therefore 'majory' in sound.) Try this sequence at the piano and the Dictionary's point will be borne out.

THE USE OF DISCRETION IN THE MINOR DIATONIC SYSTEM

Rather than getting caught up in detailing the three minor scales' raison d'etre and their various uses, there is a way to look at the minor scale system(s) that can greatly simplify the task. Essentially, the options of using F or F# and G or G# are really just that, they are options. This brings us back into the use of discretion within a harmonic system. A composer or player will learn what kinds of color these scale notes emit both in melody and as parts of chords. Think of it as different shadings available within the overall sound and color of the minor key.

This discretion works smoothly when dealing primarily with melody. Try sitting at the piano and play melodies varying between the three minor scales or combinations of the three. You can see that there are many options and one scale is not necessarily more appropriate than the other. It is in the area of building diatonic chords from the scale(s) that this discretion can create confusion. The following points clarifying the chordal structure of the minor diatonic system should be helpful.

First of all, even with the existence of the natural minor and descending melodic minor scale's b7 G note, you can assume that the predominant V chord in A minor will be E7 with its essential note G#. It is possible to make the V chord of A minor purely diatonic with the natural minor scale resulting in an E- V chord, but this is not very common[54] Another commonly used chord is the D- (or D-7) that uses the sixth note of the scale F rather than the available F#. This chord helps form the basic I IV V structure that is a foundational part of music, here expressed in minor. In our key A minor, these three chords are A-, D- and E7.

> **54.** This minor V chord can be and has been used effectively in rock and folk styles for a more pastel-like and less leading tone feel.

Play through these chords to get a sense of the fundamental quality of this sequence. Similarly, the diatonic II chord in the key of A minor, B minor 7 b5 (or B minor half diminished) consisting of the notes BDFA, is used predominantly in place of a II-7 chord which would employ the optional F#.[55]

While the above examples are useful to help clarify the common chord usages within the minor diatonic system, the examples must also give way to the impulses in music that produce the exceptions. Mainly, it is jazz and popular music that have made somewhat common use of the major 6 note within minor chords (F# in our

> **55.** A diminished chord contains notes each a minor third apart from the previous note – i.e., BDFAb. In the above example, the chord is called half diminished because the A is natural, a major third above the F, therefore breaking the diminished chain. These chords in the popular and jazz worlds are generally referred to as flat 5 chords.

Ex. 7-6

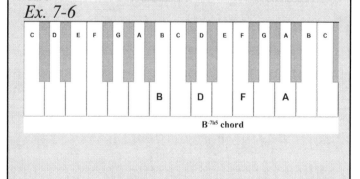

B-7b5 chord

A- example). In the IV chord in A minor this produces a D or D7 chord, and in the II chord this produces a B- or B-7. In both cases, the resulting sound is more open and a bit brighter. The A- to D7 sequence is actually very common in jazz, pop, and R&B. One example among many is Santana's song "Evil Ways" which sequences A-7 to D7 and ends the sequence by resolving an E7 chord back to A-7. An example of the use of the II-7 (again, one among many) is in the Van Morrison song "Moondance" where the keyboard vamps (plays repeatedly) from A-7 to B-7 (the B-7 containing the F#). This open sound is made that much more effective because at the release Van Morrison takes the song to the D-7 IV chord (using the F) which produces a subtle color change adding to the emotional resonance of the tune.

Stepping back to the original point of delineating the most common chord usages within the minor diatonic system, we can now start to lay out the chords I through VII as we did in the major diatonic system. The chords (starting with triads for simplicity) are as follows: A-, B° (sometimes B-), C or C augmented (the "augmented" note is the G#),[56] D- (sometimes D), E (rarely E-), and the chords on the 6th and 7th

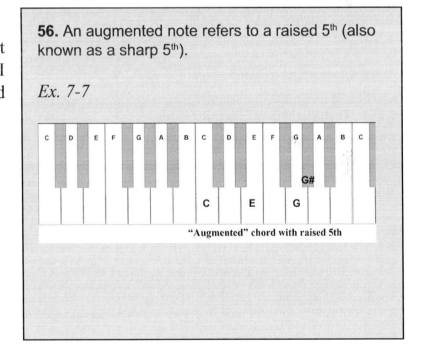

56. An augmented note refers to a raised 5th (also known as a sharp 5th).

Ex. 7-7

"Augmented" chord with raised 5th

degrees: - either F or F#° for the sixth degree and G or G#° for the seventh degree. Can you figure out where these chords come from?[57]

> **57.** The chords are diatonic in relation to the natural, melodic, and harmonic minor scales.

The use of the sixth and seventh notes comprising the VI and VII chords of the minor is flexible; there is no real fixed rule and in practice, compositionally and in improvisation, the discretion is based on melodic and chordal considerations. In the end, it is in large part based on taste and what sounds right. Of course, the art of choosing becomes refined and focused by listening, practice and experience.

One final area of discretion in the minor system needs to be looked at, that is the use of four note 7th chords. As the note options of F or F# and G or G# in the scales allow additional choices for triadic chords, this is particularly so in the area of 7th chords. Laying out the pure diatonic seventh chords for the natural minor scale (all white notes), the results are A-7, B-7 b5, C△7, D-7, E-7, F△7, G7. Taking each chord separately, the choices created by the F# and G# notes of the melodic and harmonic minor scales are: A-7 or A-△7 (there's the G#!), B-7 b5 or B-7 (F#), C△7 or C+△7, D-7 or D7 (F#), E-7 or E7 (the E7 being the most predominantly used), F△7 or F#-7 b5, G7 or G△7, and G#°7/G#-7 b5 (for now, don't worry too much about these G# chords, as this chord is essentially a function of the upper structure of the E7/V7 chord). Play through these seven chords to get a sense of the harmonic color of each. (Please see Appendix 8 for additional review of the minor diatonic triads and seventh chords.)

Ex. 7-8

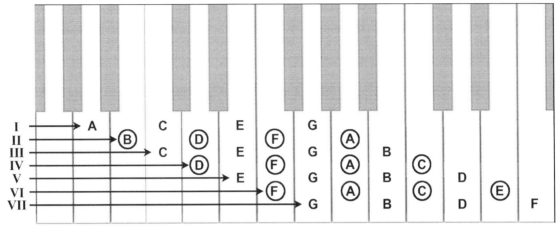

In each of the chords containing F or G there is a discretion to turn the F or G into an F# or G#. For example, the IV chord D-7 can be turned into a D7 (D F# A C).

Now finally, to give you an overall sense of the musical aesthetic and logic of the minor diatonic system, following is an analysis of the song "Black Orpheus," a popular bossa nova song from Brazil. The concepts discussed in this chapter should become more apparent and further developed within this song context. In this analysis, we will also review concepts presented earlier in this study: the V to I sequence, dominant chords, every chord has its V chord, the II V I sequence, discretionary dominant chords, sus chords, and tritone substitutions. For now, try to picture and follow the chords as written and understand how these chords fit diatonically into the various minor scales we have just reviewed. Playing through these kinds of chords will become more approachable as you work through the appendices.

Black Orpheus Chord "Changes"[58]

> [58]. Changes is a term from the jazz world — essentially a hip way of saying chord movement.

The chords for "Black Orpheus" in their entirety are:

```
| A-7       | B-7b5   E7   | A-7       | B-7b5       E7    |
| A-7       | D-7     G7   | C△7       | A7 (or C#°7)      |
| D-7       | G7           | C△7       | F△7               |
| B-7b5    | E7            | A-7       | B-7b5       E7    |

| A-7       | B-7b5   E7   | A-7       | B-7b5       E7    |
| E-7b5     | A7           | D-7       | D-7               |
| D-7       | B-7b5   E7   | A-7       | F△7               |
| B-7b5    | E7            | A-7       | B-7b5       E7    |
```

Now let's break down the chords and denote the chord numbers within the minor diatonic system.

```
| A-7       | B-7b5  E7    | A-7       | B-7b5   E7    |
| I(-7)     | II     V     | I         | II      V     |

| A-7       | D-7    G7    | C△7       | A7 (or C#°7)  |
| I         | (II    V) to the | III   | V to the      |

| D-7       | G7           | C△7       | F△7           |
| IV        | VII*         | III       | VI            |
```
* This D-7 to G7 is also a II V to C△7 as in previous line

```
| B-7b5    | E7            | A-7       | B-7b5   E7    |
| II        | V            | I         | II      V     |
```

| A-7 | B-7b5 E7 | A-7 | B-7b5 E7 |
| I(-7) | II   V | I | II   V |

| E-7b5 | A7 | D-7 | D-7 |
| II* | V to the | IV | IV |

* Notice the Bb note of the E-7b5 is not diatonic

| D-7 | B-7b5 E7 | A-7 | F△7 |
| IV | II   V | I | VI |

| B-7b5 | E7 | A-7 | B-7b5 E7 |
| II | V | I | II   V |

Now, here are alternative chord changes using some of the discretionary chords available within the minor diatonic system as well as V to Vs, tritone substitutions, sus chords, and a touch of other spice. Refer back to the original chords as needed.

| A-7 | B-7b5   E7 | A-△7   A-7 | F7 E7 |

* A-△7: from harmonic minor scale
* F7: any II V sequence can be turned into a V chord (E7 instead of B- b5 7 to E7); every chord has a V chord (B7 to E7) and F7 is the tritone substitution for B7 (or think of it simply as a dominant type chord a half step above the destination dominant chord)

| A-7 Eb7 | D-7   G7 | C△7 | E-7 A7 |

* Eb7: tritone substitution for an A7 chord leading to D-7
* E-7 A7: every V7 chord can be turned into a II V sequence

| D-7 | G7 | C△7   F#7 | F△7 |

* F#7: tritone substitution for a C7 chord leading to F△7

| B-7b5 | E7 | A-7 | B7   E7 |

* B7: dominant chord to E7 (V to a V), also considered a discretionary dominant turning the II-7 chord into a II7

| A-7 | B-7   E7 | A-7 | A-7 |

* B-7: uses F# from melodic minor scale (and it just sounds good!)
* A-7 : not every II V needs to be played

| E-7b5 | Eb7 | D-7 | D-7 |

Eb7: tritone substitution for a A7 chord leading to D-7

| D-7 | B-7b5 Bb7 | A-7 | F#-7b5 |

Bb7: tritone substitution for a E7 chord leading to A-
F#-7b5: one of the VI chords available in A minor

| B-7b5 | E7 | A-7 | Esus7 E7 |

Esus7: every II V sequence can be turned into a sus chord which can be resolved (or not)

CHAPTER VIII: INSIDE AND OUTSIDE THE DIATONIC SYSTEM

COLORING CHORDS WITH DIATONIC CHORD EXTENSIONS

The diatonic chords we have examined to this point have contained either three or four notes. We have looked at triads (i.e., C major, D minor ...) and 7th chords (i.e., C△7, D-7...). We have learned to identify the three notes of the triad as the 1st, 3rd and 5th of the chord and the four notes of the 7th chord as the 1st, 3rd, 5th, and 7th. This chapter will introduce notes that are available to play in addition to the basic notes of the triad, the seventh, or the sus chord. We will begin by looking at the available diatonic notes.

If we continued to count notes of the scale after notes 1-7 (C,D,E,F,G,A,B) and assigned numbers, the result would be as follows: the C an octave above the first C would be the 8th, D would be the 9th, E the 10th, F the 11th, G the 12th, A the 13th, and B, the 14th. The notes above the seven note scale are called "extension" notes. Since the C, E, G, and B, the notes of the C△7, are already accounted for and assigning them new numbers would be redundant, the only notes requiring identification in a C chord would be the D (9th), the F (11th), and the A (13th).

Ex. 8-1

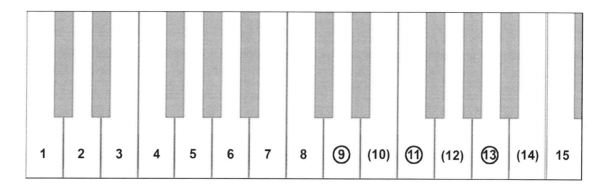

There are also times that the D, F and A notes can and should be identified as the 2nd 4th and 6th. Respectively, the D, F, and A may be called either the 2nd or the 9th, the 4th or the 11th, and the 6th or the 13th, depending on the type of chord these notes are being added to. If one of these notes is being added to a triad, the note will be deemed a 2nd, 4th, or 6th. If, in the case of C△7, a D, F, or A is being added, it will typically be labeled a 9th, 11th, or 13th. This distinction is based on the use of the 7th (the B note). The 7th in the chord gives these extension notes a quality of being an upper extension of the scale - notes higher than the seventh. On the other hand, these notes added to a triad tend to sound as the lower part of the scale, blending with the sound of the triad.

Ex. 8-2

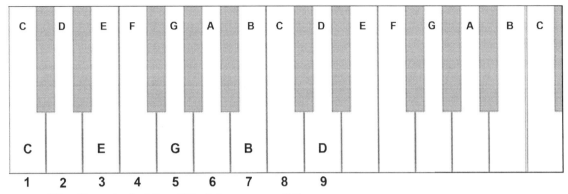

The D note is identified here as a 9th because the base chord contains a 7th. This chord would be identified as $C^{\Delta 7(9)}$.

Ex. 8-3

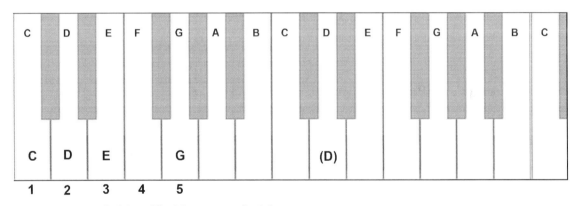

The D note is identified here as a 2nd because the base chord is a triad. This chord would be identified as C2. If the D note is to be played above the triad, some might identify this chord as C9, but this gets into an area reflecting a difference of opinion/approach towards notation. We don't need to be too concerned with this distinction.

The use of extension notes provides yet another opportunity for confusion regarding numeric identification. Actually, this is just a review of something we covered earlier. Remember that the reference here to the 1st, 3rd, 5th, 7th, and now, 2/9, 4/11 and 6/13 is a reference to the note of the chord and this does not necessarily relate to the C scale. In the above example, since I used the C△7 as the model, the notes of the chord aligned with the notes of the scale, but this is not always the case. Take for instance, the chord D-7. We can see here that the 1st, 3rd, 5th, 7th of the chord (DFAC) are not the same as the 1st, 3rd, 5th, 7th of the C major scale. Following through on this example, the 2nd/9th, 4th/11th and 6th/13th of the D-7 are E, G and B.

Ex. 8-4

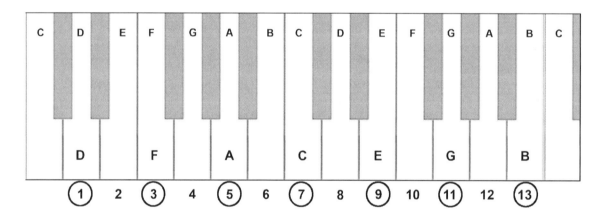

In this way, each diatonic chord of the C major scale (and of course, all scales) can be extended with diatonic notes. Whether a chord works well or not will depend on the voicing used, and the relationship of the notes within the chord. To bear out this point, if you play a C△7 and add a 9th, the result is a pleasing and quite consonant sound. Add a 13th to this chord and the sound, although perhaps a little less smoothly blended, will have some balance and logic.

Ex. 8-5

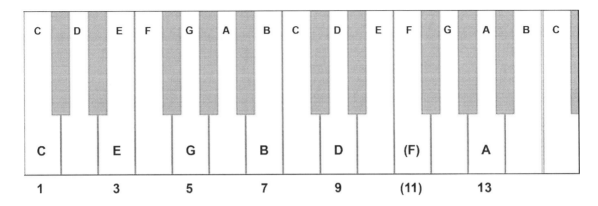

However, if one adds the 11th to a C$\triangle$7 chord, there is a striking dissonance, so much so that jazz pedagogy has labeled this note an "avoid" note within the context of the $\triangle$7 chord.[59] Understanding the ins and outs of what sounds good - what works - comes with experience and a study of specific voicings related to each of the types of chords: the major sevens, dominant sevens, minor sevens, and minor major sevens, and their extensions. Just as important, another function of these 'voicings' (the spatial placement of notes within chords) is to allow for the smoothest transition between chords, as in a II V I sequence.

> **59.** The 9th and 13th are commonly used in conjunction with seventh chords. The 11th is used less often, however, with proper care, it can be very effective.

Fortunately, jazz pedagogy has provided a systematic approach to learning these voicings and, starting only with diatonic notes, there are just a limited number of voicings to get under your belt. Please see Appendix 9 Standard Jazz Voicings for a concise study of these chords. Since you have already gotten a start on voicings using triads and seventh chords, building new chords using extension notes should be a comfortable step. Becoming familiar with these chords can take some time, but the work should serve well for those interested in developing facility on the piano. Once comfortable with the voicings and some of the typical ways in which chords move from one to another, a world of song interpretation will open itself. If this is your goal, take the time and put in the work with these exercises, they will bear fruit. For those wanting to do more advanced work and proceed into other keys, the second part of this appendix contains the voicings in keys other than C.

ALTERED CHORDS – USING NON-DIATONIC EXTENSION NOTES TO CREATE DEEPER COLORS AND A HIGHER DEGREE OF TENSION AND RELEASE

Jazz, blues, funk, pop, R&B, salsa, swing, and other styles employ 7th chords, 7th chords with diatonic extensions, and also in many cases, **7th chords with non-diatonic extension notes.** These non-diatonic notes are notes derived from the diatonic extension notes which can then be made either sharp or flat. An example of this is the V7 chord G7 in the key of C which can be expanded into a G7 chord with a 9th note A (written G7 9). This chord voiced in its 'root' position looks as follows:

Ex. 8-6

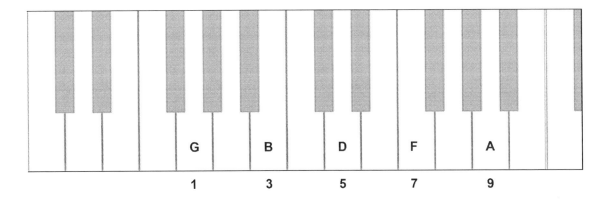

Now, in order to create a different sort of sound, the 9th note - the A - can be made either sharp or flat. The result is either a #9 (A#) or a b9 (Ab). The G7 b9 in its root position looks as follows:

Ex. 8-7

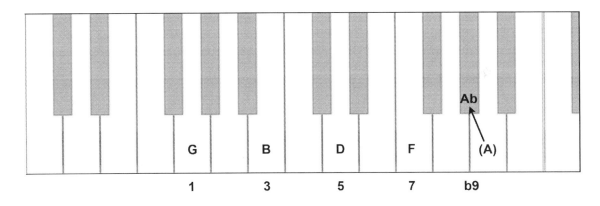

The significance of these non-diatonic extension notes is that, first, they help create a richer and more dissonant sound, a type of dissonance that can be satisfying as in the hot and unusual spices flavoring an exotic meal. The food analogy is apt because in certain styles of music, using only diatonic notes when working through the chords can create a rather bland result in the same way that food without salt, garlic, and other spices is not very exciting. So here, in addition to extending 7th chords with a nice diatonic 9th, 11th (where appropriate), or 13th, the spice rack can now include the b9, #9, 11, #11, and b13.[60] In Appendix 10 - Altered Jazz Chords, you can see examples of the kinds of chords that work well and are commonly used. Because of the additional options created between the use of diatonic and non-diatonic extensions notes and the choice of where to place these notes (voicings), there are also opportunities to create some unusual and evocative chords. Mining the beauty available in these types of chords is part of the challenge in the study and application of jazz harmony. Some of these chords are set out in the appendix.

> **60.** There is no need and use for a b11 or #13 because these notes are already accounted for: in the chord G7, a b11 would be a B (the third of the chord) and a #13 would be an F (the seventh of the chord).

There is perhaps an even more significant purpose for the use of non-diatonic extension notes in chords, at least from the perspective of a large theme of this book. One of the main concepts of this study has been the idea that harmony is based on a diatonic system that can be expanded into the non-diatonic world primarily through the use of dominant chords and dominant type chords or notes that work as tension and release mechanisms. **Non-diatonic extension notes are another means of creating this tension and release, a tension and release that is based on the fundamental principal we have already discussed, the inherent pull from notes a half step apart.** As it turns out, non-diatonic notes in all cases happen to be a half step away from a diatonic note. Consider the diatonic notes in the key of C major: C, D, E, F, G, A, B, C. All of the remaining notes C#/Db, D#/Eb, F#/Gb, G#/Ab, A#/Bb are each a half step away from a diatonic note in the C scale.

Ex. 8-8

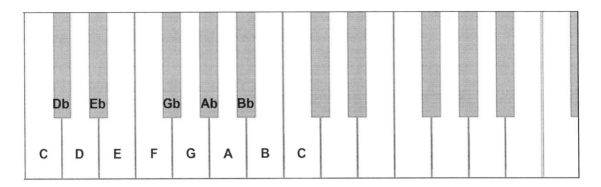

This in effect gives these notes a dominant type role with respect to the diatonic note a half step away. These non-diatonic extension notes when used in chords typically resolve within the chord itself, or within the chord sequence.

To make things clearer and for the purpose of review, remember that the tri-tone substitution chord (i.e., a Db7 replacing a G7) functions as a dominant type chord not only because its 7th and 3rd is a mirror image of the 3rd and 7th of the V7 G7 chord, but because its root note is a half step away from the destination chord. (The root note Db of the tritone substitution chord is a half step away from the root note C of the C chord.)

Ex. 8-9

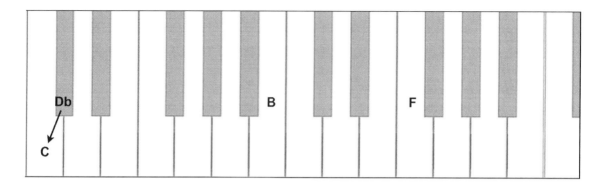

As we have already seen, this kind of half step relationship is in large part the driving force in the V to I relationship. (The 3rd and 7th of the V chord each move a half step to the 1st and 3rd of the I chord.)

Ex. 8-10

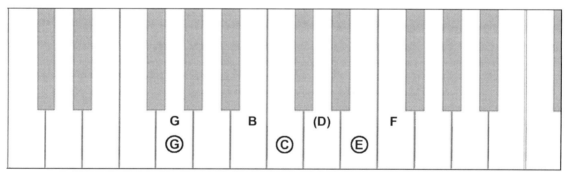

V to I

Just as the half step movement drives the tension and release in the dominant and dominant type chords, and a half step relationship between root notes creates attraction, **non-diatonic extension notes a half step away from the diatonic serve as mini-dominants to the resolving destination note**. A more broad way to understand this concept is to consider all of the diatonic

108   Western Harmony Simplified

tones of the scale, at least to some degree, to be a sort of home base, a destination for the non-diatonic notes a half step away.[61]

> **61.** This is an important yet simple concept because once one becomes familiar with the diatonic notes within a scale (in our case, the notes of C major), the non-diatonic notes are easily distinguishable and, at least, theoretically, a quick learn. Another way to think of it is that you are always only one half step away from a 'correct' diatonic note. Even this 'incorrect' note is not 'wrong,' because it can always be resolved! Further, these notes are not just useful to color chords, but because of their quality to resolve to diatonic notes, they can be used very effectively for melodic embellishment. Think Chopin, bebop, blues ...

Let's take a closer look at how extension notes can serve as mini-dominants. Suppose we take a G7 13 chord voiced as follows: GFBE.[62] In anticipating this chord's resolution to C△7 9, I might choose to keep the G, F, and B in place as I move the E to an Eb and then resolve this chord GFBEb (a G7 b13) to a C△7 9 voiced as CEBD.

> **62.** The player has the discretion to leave out the 5th of the chord because it is not an important note with respect to defining the chord. This is a somewhat common practice in voicing chords except when dealing with the X-7 b5 where the 5 is playing a strong defining role (indicating a minor key).

Ex. 8-11

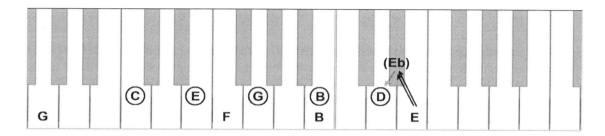

If you play this on piano, you might notice a few things. First, the E of the G7 13, though consonant to a degree, also stands out pretty well, and its movement to Eb comes as a relief of sorts. The following movement and resolution of the Eb to D as the G7 b13 chord moves to C△7 9 is also a welcome release of tension created by the Eb non-diatonic note moving to the diatonic tone D of the C△7 9 chord. (And lets not forget the 7th note F of the G7 chord resolves to the E of the C△7 9 chord creating a double barreled tension and release.)

In the above example, you may have noticed I alluded to the tension and release between the E and Eb of the G7 chord without explaining how a *diatonic extension* creates tension and release. Generally, there will be a definite pull between the non-diatonic to the diatonic notes a half step away, but it also can work the other way. With this 'anomaly,' two things are going on. The first is very simple, that is - notes a half step apart have an inherent pull towards each other which is either heightened or lessened depending on the context. The context in the case of the G7 13 to G7 b13 to C△7 9 movement is that the E note 13 of the G7 chord is somewhat exposed because there are no other notes within close proximity to shade its presence. Further along this line, this E is quite dissonant when played only against the 7th note F below, even though it is shaded by the B note 3rd of the chord played in between. In any case, a diatonic extension note (the E) can serve as a mini-dominant to a non-diatonic extension note (the Eb) which can then serve as a mini-dominant to a resolving note within the following chord (the D in the C△7 9). This is, in a manner of speaking, another example of a V to a V type relationship. Try this above example on the piano, and the explanation should become clear.

In another example, we can even take this idea of a V to a V or dominant to dominant type relationship further. Suppose instead of a G7 13 chord, we start with a G7 13,#9 voiced as follows: GFBEA#.

Ex. 8-12

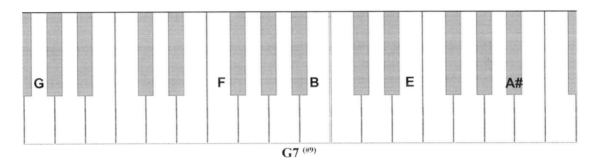

The movement towards the C△7 9 I might choose would be to resolve the A# to A to Ab and on to G of the C chord. This in effect creates a V to V to V (let's call them "mini Vs") by way of the half step tension and release movement. I might also choose to resolve the E of the G7 to Eb which could then resolve to the D, the 9th of the C chord. The chord sequence would look as follows: GFBEA# to GFBEA to GFBEbAb to CEBDG.

Ex. 8-13

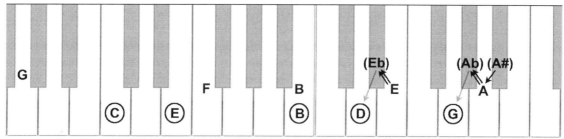

G7 with non-diatonic extensions resolving to $C^{\Delta 7(9)}$

This example may appear somewhat complicated, but the important point is to see yet again the power of the half step relationship between notes, and how in the context of extension notes, this pull can be used very effectively. Play through this last example to get a sense of the color and movement that is possible through the use of extension notes, both non-diatonic and diatonic. (Playing this sequence is easiest to do by playing G and F in the left hand and the other three notes in the right.)

A closer look at extensions is provided in Appendix 10. There you will find commonly used chords that provide familiar harmonic color to jazz, funk, neo-soul, the sweet harmony of Brazilian bossa nova, and pop music. One example of these chords is the #9 which is used commonly in jazz (often with other extension notes), but is also very recognizable as a funk or James Brown kind of chord.

Ex. 8-14

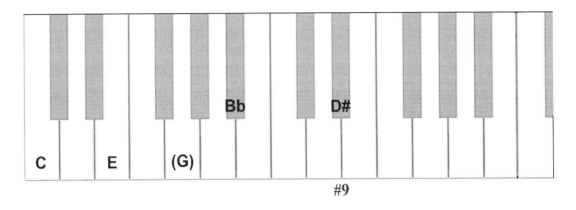

It is by developing familiarity with these types of recognizable chords (as well as by seeking out the less common chords) that will allow you to become fluent in more advanced harmony. Play through the chords in the appendix and try to relate these chords to sounds you have heard and to what appeals to you aesthetically. Take the time to understand the relationship of the extended notes within the chords. Your efforts will be rewarded with a more fundamental grasp of the harmonic system.

Finally, a word of caution as well as encouragement. A rote coloring of chords without a good sense of an underlying aesthetic can lead to an overuse of extensions, a strange balance of complex and simple chords, ineffective or non-existent voice leading, and tensions unresolved or too obviously resolved. Of course, improvement in this area will come with experience, but here are some general points to keep in mind, some broad concepts I have become aware of through my playing and listening travels.[63] First, don't over spice! One of the things I have learned, particularly from jazz great Bill Evans, is that a proper voicing of a simple chord can be the most perfect choice. There may be a temptation to add multiple extensions to a chord, whereas a simple three note chord perhaps with a 3, 7, and 13 might be the most musical. Even in this latter example, a b13 could be chosen instead of the natural 13 (or in another case a 9 or a b9). Understanding the subtle impact of these choices is what separates players. On a less subtle but related point, over spicing can lead to just that - over spicing. Imagine going to a Greek restaurant and eating grape leaves, a salad doused in vinegar, hummus with lots of garlic, no bread, a martini with olives, rice with an abundant amount of salt, spiced radishes and no tzatziki (a yogurt dish) and then skip desert. You'd probably feel that you weren't eating a well balanced meal and tire of it quickly. In this way, watch for the overuse of the b9 or b13 resolution to a chordal tone, as too much of these sequences can quickly turn the harmony into an unappetizing mix. Again, it is sensitivity to the impact of the choices that makes a difference.

> **63.** Don't forget how important it is to listen to musicians who have developed this aesthetic. You can't go wrong with starting with the some of the greats of jazz piano: Bill Evans, Keith Jarrett, Oscar Peterson, Herbie Hancock with Miles Davis, and on the more sparse side of things you might try the trio recordings of John Lewis (founder of the Modern Jazz Quartet), Thelonious Monk and Horace Silver (for a little bit of funky edge). I also shouldn't leave out the non-jazz pianists who have mastered the art of the right voicing with just the appropriate amount of spice, (and, for the most part, using non-diatonic notes only sparingly) – pianist songwriters like Carole King, Joni Mitchell, Billy Joel, Elton John, and others …

An antidote to this over spicing is to use fewer non-diatonic notes. You might choose to voice a V7 chord with a natural 9th and/or 13th rather than a non-diatonic extension note in order to *avoid* too much of a feeling of tension and release. This helps to keep the music more open in feeling. A final related point: keeping the music more open, more pastel in quality, can be achieved by using a sus chord in place of the V7, especially if the sus chord is left unresolved. A sus chord is naturally an open sounding chord because of the absence of the 3rd. Another step in this direction is to limit discretionary dominant chords and in their place use a sus chord. A II V sequence where both chords are sus chords goes a long way to producing this open effect. Again, all these choices are made within the context of the feeling and style of the music, what is going on with the other musicians in the ensemble, and where your emotions are taking you as a player. The catalogue of your choices over time becomes your style.

CHAPTER IX: THE BLUES - WHERE THE DOMINANT IS KING

There have been many books written about the history and origins of the "blues." This chapter will not deal with the origins of this music as much as the harmonic structure of the blues, its effect on various styles, and, mostly, its harmonic relationship to the diatonic system laid out so far. Suffice it to say with regard to the importance of blues, it is a style that permeates American popular music, its influence stretching in countless directions. Without blues, there would be no Beatles, Rolling Stones, Jimi Hendrix, the Allman Brothers, and much of Bob Dylan's work. Without blues, we would not have had the pleasure of hearing the great blues artists like B.B. King, Albert King, Muddy Waters, and John Lee Hooker. Without blues, the entire history of jazz would have been different if not completely absent, and the black sound of MoTown and Philadelphia would never have existed. And finally, without blues, countless musicians (including myself) would have missed the opportunity to steep themselves in a roots tradition that provides a real and immediate language to spontaneously express emotion through music.

The basic language of blues is quite simple – the blues progressions use the I IV and V chord and at times only one or two of these chords. In my musical life, I was able to take to this style as a young musician, not only because it touched my musical soul, but because learning the form did not require the kind of musical sophistication inherent in learning more advanced styles of jazz. I recommend a study of this style of music because it will help provide a strong foundation to the kinds of harmonic structures we have discussed to this point. At its root, simple, the blues form also evolved within itself and as transformed through Jazz, R&B, and Soul, into a rather sophisticated harmonic language that can fully employ the kinds of diatonic and non-diatonic elements of harmony we have been discussing.[64]

> **64.** For the basic outline of the '12 bar blues,' please see Appendix 11 - the Blues. Start initially with the simple 12 bar form and refer to the more evolved examples as the information in this chapter becomes more clear.

THE BLUES SCALE

An important vehicle within blues that can make the idiom approachable to a less sophisticated musician is the blues scale which in large part defines the style.[65] The early blues scale used (and still uses) the notes C, Eb/E, F, G/Gb, and Bb.

> **65.** Care needs to be taken with this idea and significance of the less "sophisticated" musician. Essentially this term refers to someone with less technical training and is not meant pejoratively. If you've ever heard a well trained classical musician try to 'swing' or play blues who doesn't have the experience or feel, this not only can sound unsophisticated, but downright silly. Sophistication is, of course, relative to context.

Ex. 9-1

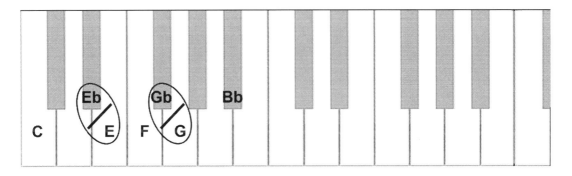

This five note scale is also referred to as a pentatonic scale.[66] The source of this blues scale was the vocal expressions of the African-American slaves working in the fields. These field hollers and work songs of the slaves were unaccompanied so, at least initially, the blues was formed out of this monophonic melodic expression. The sense of these notes being the primary and necessary voice of the blues, more than the harmonic accompaniment, still exists today. As we will see, however, the harmony of blues evolved and, at its best, can have an emotional richness and at times complexity without losing the basic primal feel of the blues sound.

> **66.** A pentatonic scale is a scale containing five notes. This can refer to a five note scale other than the blues scale, however, within the context of popular music, the pentatonic often refers to the scale for the blues.

The notes of the blues scale are also significant because, not surprisingly, they provide the foundational material for the underlying harmony. Probably the most significant impact the blues pentatonic scale has had on blues harmony is the effect created by the use of the 3rd and 7th of the scale. The existence of the b7 in the scale inclines the I chord of the blues (in the case of C) to be a C7 rather than a C△7. The C7 chord in effect becomes the diatonic chord within the context of the C blues scale: C, Eb/E, F, G/Gb, and Bb.

118   Western Harmony Simplified

Ex. 9-2

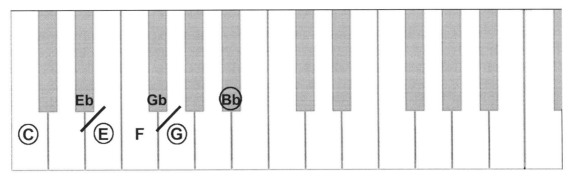

**C, E, G and Bb are the diatonic notes of C7
in the C blues system**

Following this idea further, the IV chord of the blues becomes an F7 (using the Eb) unlike the F△7 which is diatonic to the C major scale. These diatonic connections are not as clear when dealing with the V7 G7 chord of the blues which uses the notes GBDF, rather than GBbDF, which would appear be the more diatonic (with respect to the blues scale) of the 2 chords. From a musical perspective, the reason for the use of the dominant seven chord is clear; it is the same as in the use of the dominant V7 chord in the major or minor scale: the chordal structure of the dominant chord provides the tension release mechanism for the return to the I chord. In addition to this tension release purpose, G7 is by itself a stronger harmonic color than the G minor 7 when played against the blues scale.

We should also keep in mind that the discussion about diatonicism, as applied to the blues, is an after the fact construct. The bottom line is that if something sounds right, that's reason enough, there's no need to explain everything, and in some cases, explanation is futile. In this way, the blues scale as it is performed in real life is not fully and explainably diatonic to the underlying harmony. Notice that the scale for the blues contains C, **Eb/E**, F, **G/Gb**, and Bb. The reason for using the two notes **Eb/E** and **G/Gb** to identify the 3rd and 5th is that these 'blue' notes are hard to identify with the fixed scale notes of Western music. The blues originated as an oral tradition so the notes chosen were not based by default on a 'fixed' pitch. The early performers found that sometimes notes in-between Eb and E and the Gb and G were the most effective for expressing the crying emotion that is typical of the blues. One of the reasons the guitar became such a strong blues instrument is its ability to affect the sound of the human voice and, through the bending of the strings, access these difficult to define blue notes.

Apart from the visceral effect of the blues scale itself, the blue notes combined with the harmonic base of dominant chords can create uniquely sensual and powerful emotional textures. The Eb/E blue note 3rd of the scale supported by a C7 chord is the typical sound of the blues. The resulting chord here is a C7#9 which we saw earlier is a commonly used chord within the R&B, Soul, and Jazz idioms.

Ex. 9-3

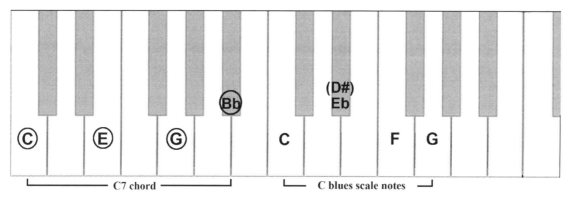

Results in a C$^{7\#9}$ chord

The G/Gb 5th of the scale against the chords creates a spice that a straight G would not create. The Bb of the blues scale against the C7 is the 7th which in itself we have seen is a strong tension note. Against the F7 chord, this Bb is quite dissonant and in some circles might be considered an "avoid" note.[67]

Against a G7 chord, the Bb is the #9, another instance of this strong harmonic chord.

> **67.** The blues scale has a strong identity and self contained power that allows for flexibility when its individual notes are played atop the underlying chords. The Bb would often be played as part of a blues phrase that is strong enough to survive the passing dissonance over an F7 chord. For the adventurous musician, a confident stressing of this note in this context could work very effectively.

Ex. 9-4

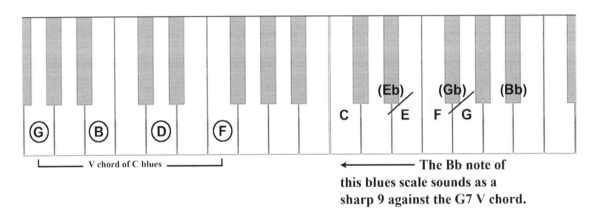

The Bb note of this blues scale sounds as a sharp 9 against the G7 V chord.

A big part of learning to play blues is to feel the impact that each of the notes of the scale has against the chords that make up the blues progression.

Western Harmony Simplified

Composers in the blues idiom often use this idea by creating a "riff"[68] of one or more notes that would be played rhythmically against the movement of chords underneath. The notes of the riff have a different effect as they are repeated on top of the varying chords. Two other quick points on this topic: first, the choice of where the blue note 3rd is placed pitchwise will effect the harmonic result. Yes, the 3rd as a note close to Eb will create a C7#9 chord, but a performer may feel this note closer to the E, which will change the sound of the C7 chord. Similarly, and second point, the same is true as this Eb/E is played over an F7 chord or G7 chord. The choice of pitch will affect the nature of the overall chord. This point will be expanded and clarified below as well as in Appendix 11 - The Blues.

> **68.** A melodic phrase, usually short in length. A great example of this is Duke Ellington's classic "C Jam Blues."

THE BLUES AND THE DIATONIC

In spite of the unique aspects and incongruities of applying the blues scale to its chord structure, there remain strong points of connection with the diatonic system we have been studying. In fact, the chords of the C blues and the C major scale diatonic systems contain the same roots: the I, II, III, IV, V, VI, and VII chords share the roots C, D, E, F, G, A and even B. Although the E and B of these chords at first glance do not appear purely diatonic to the blues scale, an argument can be made that the E is one of the notes of the blues scale and that the B is merely a root of a diminished chord which is a form of G7. The fact that the blues diatonic system shares the roots of chords with C major makes it easier for us to apply many of the concepts we have learned to this point: every chord has a dominant that can lead to it, every chord can have a II V leading to it, the tritone substitution chord can replace any of these V chords, and V chords and II V sequences can be turned into sus chords.[69]

> **69.** There are some blues styles that incorporate chords with roots more directly related to the pentatonic blues scales. These styles tend to fall into the rock and pure blues genres and less towards jazz. For the purpose of exploring the relationship of the blues with the diatonic system, we are going to focus now on the blues/jazz connection.

One of the most commonly used principals in blues and its related styles is the use of discretionary dominant chords, another concept we examined in the C major diatonic system. In the blues system where, as the chapter heading says "the dominant is king," the discretionary dominants feel very much at home. In the more simple forms of blues where the I IV and V chords are predominantly used, there is not as much opportunity to incorporate the discretionary dominants (i.e., the II, III and VI chords) and to hear their effect. As blues progressed and influenced other styles, the II, III and VI chords became more widely used and I would hazard to say, in their use, were more often than not played as discretionary dominants. The blues is a powerful form where one note can vibrate with intensity. This is an intensity that never quite resolves; the use of the discretionary dominants helps to keep this flame at the right burn.

The blues appendix lays out how the blues progression evolved to use the II, III, and VI chords as well as V to Vs, II Vs, tritone substitutions, and sus chords. Becoming fluent with the more complex blues forms can take some time. The best approach to developing in this area is to first become completely comfortable with the structure of the blues in its most simple form (most often 12 bars)[70] where only the I IV and V chords are used. Improvise with the blues scales against this progression until it becomes second nature. Once this is achieved, follow the evolution laid out in the appendix step by step.

Western Harmony Simplified   123

> **70.** A bar, also referred to as a "measure," is a measurement of musical time. Within the blues, this bar typically contains 4 beats.

Another useful exercise to get a sense of the blues scale and how it relates to the underlying harmony is to play the chords in the left hand (using either the 1st and 7th note or 3rd and 7th notes as voicings) and improvise playing the blues scale in the right hand. With the blues progression incorporating the discretionary dominants, you will get a sense of how the notes of the blues scale color the underlying harmony. (We already looked at this, for example, with the Eb/E being played against the C7 chord creating a #9.) The resulting combinations between the blues scale and the discretionary dominants is one of the things that gives the blues its 'juice'. For example, a blues line using the C descending through Bb and G played over a E7 will have a particular sound, as will this riff played over an A7 or D7. The notes of this and other riffs within the blues scale result in dominant chords with different types of extensions.

Ex. 9-5

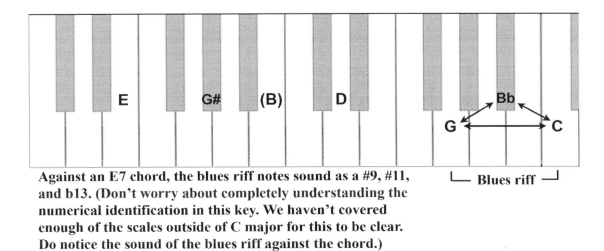

Against an E7 chord, the blues riff notes sound as a #9, #11, and b13. (Don't worry about completely understanding the numerical identification in this key. We haven't covered enough of the scales outside of C major for this to be clear. Do notice the sound of the blues riff against the chord.)

Ex. 9-6

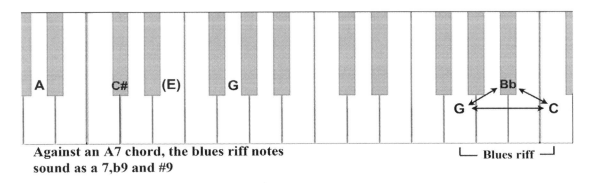

Against an A7 chord, the blues riff notes sound as a 7, b9 and #9

These examples show why the dominants tend to be used in blues instead of the minor seven II, III and VI chords, which are not as receptive to the kinds of extensions formed by the blues notes. In any event, with these dominants, there are all kinds of combinations available; choose wisely and in the meantime look through the appendix for a more complete analysis and outline. And, most of all, don't forget to acquire a grounding in the roots of the music which comes through listening and any kind of exposure that may be available.

Western Harmony Simplified

Two final points on the subject of blues harmony need to be made before moving on to the next chapter. First, the preceding discussion regarding approaches one can take to blues, that of incorporating the concepts from the C major diatonic system, works the other way as well. In other words, **the sound of the blues – the result of the blues scale and the tendency toward dominant chords can be brought back into material that is fundamentally based on a major diatonic system**. Here, one of the primary connecting points between these two systems is the use of the discretionary dominants. For example, if one were playing a song that had the chords C△7 to D-7 to G7 back to C△7 (I to II to V to I), changing the D-7 to D7 would in effect turn a diatonic majory sound into more of a blues sound. Whether a blues scale is then used on top of this progression is up to the performer - how 'bluesy' one wants to get. This connection has a little bit of the chicken or the egg syndrome. Do the discretionary dominants in the major system lead to the blues sound, or does the inclination towards a blues sound lead toward the discretionary dominants? Probably, these two things cannot be separated, only proving that the blues is a fundamental ingredient of the various jazz and jazz influenced styles of music.

The second point before moving on - the minor diatonic system also has its related blues system, not surprisingly called the "**minor blues**." Details of this system are set out in the appendix but the fundamentals are pretty much the same as in the 'major' blues.[71] The minor blues uses the same basic 12 bar structure as the major blues, the same dominant V chord, and allows for Vs and II Vs leading to destination chords, tritone substitutions, sus chords, and again, discretionary dominants. The use of the different 6th and 7th notes

---

71. Using the term 'major' blues is just a way to distinguish here between the blues based on the dominant chords and the blues based on minor 7 chords. Typically, the term blues references the C7 type blues. In most cases, specifying a "major" blues is not necessary. Reference, however, to a "minor" blues is common.

in the minor scales creates for more melodic and chordal options than in the major blues. Harmonically, the minor blues uses the C-7 and F-7 as the I and IV (with some variations), a very different sound than the C7 and F7 of the major blues. In addition to the harmonic/diatonic foundation, the minor blues sets itself apart further from the major by its use of the minor 3rd only (the Eb) in the blues scale, not the flexible Eb/E of the 'major' blues. The minor blues scale is otherwise the same as in the major blues; only the E note is avoided as it would create too much of a dissonance against the C-7.[72]

72. As in most cases of rules or avoid notes, exceptions can be created: The E note against the C-7 would stick out and rarely be used. However, the E note might be workable when played against the V7 chord (G7) of the C- blues progression. This E would be the 13 of the G7 chord which could be resolved through the Eb to D (or left unresolved). The E in this case is not serving so much as part of the blues scale as it is an extended note of the G7 chord. In this way, in the more advanced forms of blues and blues inflected styles, many notes outside the blues scale are prone to make an appearance. These kinds of harmonic devices are covered in more depth in the Blues Appendix.

Ex. 9-7

A possible V7 chord in the C minor blues

CHAPTER X: MODES

FORMING NEW TONAL CENTERS FROM THE MAJOR SCALE

In Western harmony, modes are essentially seven note scales built from a given key (in our case, C major). Each mode evokes a different harmonic color. In the key of C (and in the other 11 keys) there are 7 modes, each of these 7 modes built by starting the 'root' note of the mode on one of the seven notes of the major scale. By changing the bass or home note of the scale but still using the notes of C major for the scale material, whole harmonic palettes are derived that can be used for songs, improvisation, or, as we will examine in more detail, chord formation and coloring.

The names of the modes starting on the C and continuing through the notes of the C major scale are as follows: the scale starting on the 1st note of C major (note C): Ionoian; the scale starting on the 2nd note of C major (note D): Dorian; E: Phrygian; F: Lydian; G: Mixolydian; A: Aeolian; and, B: Locrian.

Ex. 10-1

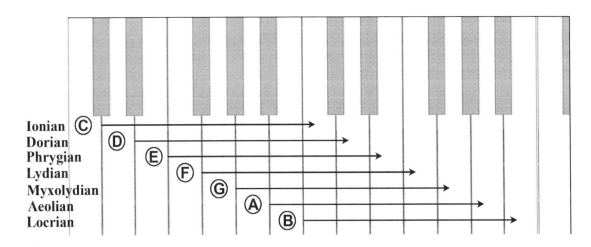

Try to play through each of these modes. By playing either the scales directly, or playing any of the notes of the scale in the right hand and playing the root note in the left hand, you'll hear that each scale/mode has a unique flavor. And again there's good news – just as we've been using the C major scale as our diatonic base in part because of the predominance of white notes, these white notes also make learning and playing modes easier. Feel free to improvise on any of these modes using the left hand as a drone on the root note, and using the right hand to play any of the notes available in whatever combinations might arise. (Go for it, the notes are all white; they can't be missed!) This is a great exercise for musicians who have trouble improvising because the modes provide source material that does not require extensive technical knowledge or experience with different types of chords; all that is required is knowledge of one scale.[73]

73. Miles Davis' classic album Kind of Blue features the cut "So What" which is an exploration of one of these modes - Dorian (D, E, F, G, A, B, C, (D)). Here, the bass player centers his 'walking" notes around the D root note and the musicians improvise using the notes of the C major scale.

Western Harmony Simplified

It's important in understanding this kind of modal playing that - in our example of C major - this scale is only providing the material for the modes; the resulting mode (for example D Dorian as in Miles Davis' "So What") is entirely independent from C major other than its use of the notes of that scale. The musicians on "So What" are playing in a mode; their home base is D and the sound of the Dorian mode, which happens to be minor. It is possible that some improvisers may play this Dorian scale by thinking a C major scale over a D bass note, but this is somewhat of a crutch. A player will generally have a stronger connection to the feel and material of the modes by hearing them independently from the root of the scale material from which it is derived.

Let's take a look at some other examples of the formation of modes to solidify our understanding of this concept. This time we'll use a G major scale as the source material (remember - G major has one sharp note: GABCDEF#G). The Lydian scale starts on the 4th note of the source major scale; in the key of G, that would be note C. *(See Ex. 10-1).* The resulting scale is CDEF#GABC.

Ex. 10-2

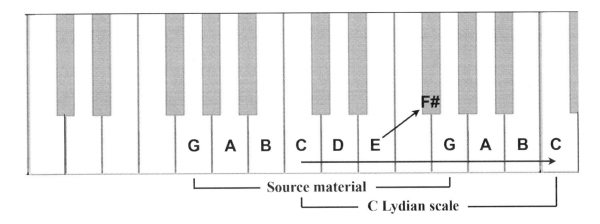

Notice that the scale material of this mode is the same as in the G major scale. If you play this scale independently from thinking G major, however, the scale takes on an entirely different character (make sure the root note in the left hand is C). Let's look at another mode example going back to the C major scale for the source material. The Phrygian mode's scale starts on the 3rd note of the source major scale. In the C major scale, that would be note E. The resulting scale is EFGABCDE.

Ex. 10-3

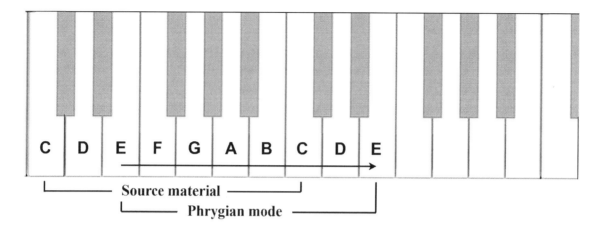

Here again, the scale material is the C major scale, but by putting E in the bass, the unique independent character of the Phrygian mode becomes clear.

MODES - A NEW APPROACH TO CHORD FORMATION AND COLORING

A somewhat different 'take' on the modes is to use them to broaden our imagination with respect to the chordal palette of a diatonic system. This approach incorporates one of the main themes of this book, that is - by becoming familiar with the major scale, we can then easily 'see' the chordal material making up that diatonic system.[74] Similarly, with the modes, once you become familiar with a given major scale, the modes that are derived from

---

74. To review further: by continuously looking at the C major scale, its diatonic chords by now probably have become quite familiar. As you approach new keys, all the concepts we learned for the C major diatonic system will apply in the same way. All that will be required will be to become familiar in sight and feel with the new scale that makes up the key.

that scale material should be easily recognized. This ease of recognition applies to the above section on using modes to create new tonal centers, and now will also apply to our application of modes within the diatonic chord systems.[75]

75. Once the source scale is learned, the associated modes will become clear. Now, to shed some light on this further: what is the 6th note of the C major scale? Answer: A. This A is the first note of the Aeolian mode using the C major scale material. What is the 6th note of the F major scale? Answer: D. This D is the first note of the Aeolian mode using the F major scale note material.

Ex. 10-4

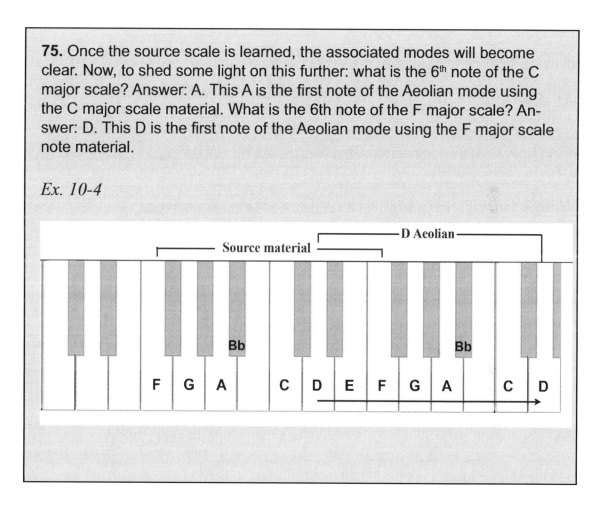

By incorporating modes back into a diatonic system, we are essentially doing the opposite of what was explained above - that each mode is independent of the source material but for its sharing of notes. The difference here is that for this new application of modes, we are going to presume we are working in a diatonic system and not so much using the modes for their particular color. Essentially, we will be looking at our C major scale model,

Western Harmony Simplified   133

seeing it as a mode (which it is – the Ionian), and how each chord of its diatonic system can be constructed from this 'modal' material. This is primarily a visual and tactile sense of scale material that works wonders for incorporating modal thinking into the building of chords, particularly chords that are colored by diatonic extension notes.[76]

> **76.** As covered earlier, diatonic extension notes are notes that are added to triadic or 7th chords. For example: A 'C' triad contains CEG and a C△7 contains CEGB. The notes D and A are extension notes from the scale that can extend the basic 7th chord.

The operative concept here, one that greatly simplifies things, is that we will use only *one mode* to color the diatonic system. This approach is unlike many harmony books and systems that discuss the various modes to be considered when improvising over the chords of a diatonic system. I believe this approach creates unnecessary steps. The basic idea of this 'encumbered' approach is that for example, if you were in C major and playing on the G7 V chord, you would 'think' of the Mixolydian scale. (Remember: the Mixolydian starts on the 5th note of the root scale, here C major, creating the scale G,A,B,C,E,D,F,G). Similarly, if you were on the F IV chord, you would 'think' of the Lydian scale. Ok, this is fine, and accurate to a degree, but here is what is unnecessary: <u>as long as you are playing diatonically, the only 'mode' that needs to be dealt with is the original C major scale (the Ionian mode)</u>. The end result will be the same because the G Mixolydian, F Lydian and C major scales share the same notes. This is yet another example of how familiarizing yourself with the basic major scale will go a long way towards an understanding of the diatonic (and modal) systems that follow.

Ex. 10-5

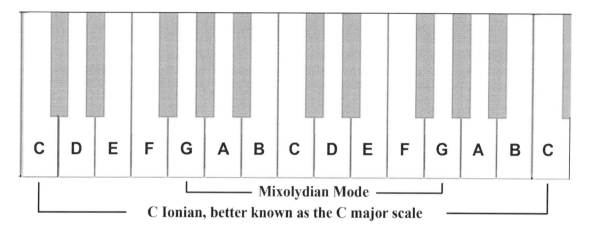

Familiarity with the scale simplifies chord formation, especially if we 'see' the C scale as a mode. In this modal approach, we can start to see the scale beyond individual notes and the individual chords, and instead see the scale as a whole, almost as one splash of color. You might have had a sense of this approach when we examined modes as individual colors independent of a diatonic system as in the E Phrygian or F Lydian. When improvising on these modes, it can be very easy to see/hear these modes as a 'splash of color' by playing a root note (E in the case of Phrygian) and literally using your arm or a rolling fist to play 'clusters' of notes. We can also do this by using C as the root note and playing clusters of white notes above that – the sound of C Ionian. Now, we can take this approach, this clustery splash of color idea, and incorporate it into the formation of chords.

Let's start by focusing on this C Ionian cluster idea and imagine that, instead of just a splash of color, we will actually be forming a chord of some sort. Let's assume for now that since the C is the root/bass note, the chord will be some kind of C chord. What chord will this form? If we played every note within our cluster (easy to do if you use your forearm to create the cluster), you would end up with a chord with the following notes: **C** as the root with a splash of D, **E**, F, **G**, A, and **B**.

Ex. 10-6

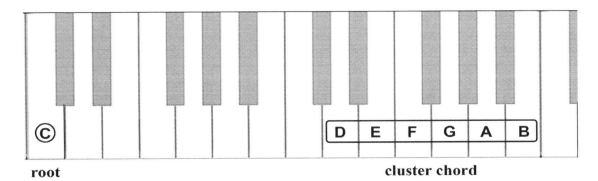

root   cluster chord

We can see that this chord contains the notes 1, 3, 5 and 7 which form the C△7 chord (CEGB). The other notes in this cluster, D, F, and A, based on our understanding of diatonic extension notes would be labeled as the 9th (D), the 11th (F), and the 13th (A). Accordingly, we could call this chord, C△7 (9, 11, 13).[77]

> **77. Identifying Chords** — This is a very important point: when trying to describe a given group of notes as a chord, look for the simplest chord and build from there. Start with the root (lowest) note and see if a major or minor triad can be built on top of that. The simplest chord is a triad and the next simplest would be the addition of the 7th note of the chord. This is fundamental chord formation and will go a long way to make chord recognition easier. In the above example, because of the context of having the root note C in the bass, I first looked for a chord with C as the root and found the C major triad (CEG). I then looked for a seventh and found the B. It theoretically
> (Continued)

> would have been possible to call this chord E-7 because it contains the notes E,G,B, and D, but this label would be unnecessarily complex because of the C in the bass. Again, first look to see if there is a triad (major or minor) that can be built upon the root/base note, then, a seventh and then build the rest of the chord from there. (There may be times when a major triad in root position can not be formed over the lowest tone of the chord. We will examine this situation shortly.)
>
> One other point in review: the D, F and A notes of the C△7 (9,11,13) could theoretically be labeled as the 2nd, 4th and 6th. However, as previously covered, when there is a 7th note in a chord, any 'extension' notes will generally be labeled as notes numerically above that seventh. These notes tend to sound literally as notes 'extended' above the seventh, thus their labeling as 'extension' notes.

Now, let's play A as the root/bass note with a white note cluster on top. The resulting 'chord' is **A** in the bass along with the notes. B,**C**,D,**E**,F,**G**.

Ex. 10-7

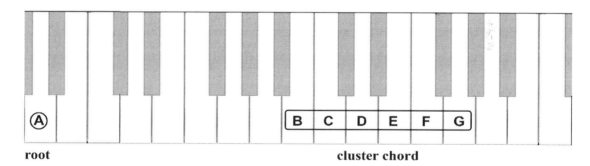

root   cluster chord

Using the system of chord identification described in comment 77, we can find a triadic chord: A minor (ACE). We then look for a seventh, which produces the chord ACEG or A-7. In addition, we have the notes B, D, and F that need to be accounted for. The resulting chord name is A-7 (9, 11, b13).

Western Harmony Simplified

If we try this again using D as the root along with the cluster splash, we get D in the bass along with the notes E,**F**,G,**A**,B, and **C**, otherwise know as D-7 (9, 11, 13).

The point of this process is to illustrate how easy it is make rich chords by filling in the notes of any chord with the notes of the major scale that defines that diatonic system. Once familiar with the scale source, it is almost a matter of just splashing in color from that scale, which is already familiar to the eye and touch. We already saw how this is done on the three chords above; we can color the III chord (E-), IV chord (F), and V chord (G) in the same way. This, of course, will work in other keys as well.

The above should seem quite simple, and, for the most part, it is. There is a glitch in this process, however, that we need to deal with. By using that most important sense - the ear - in addition to the visual and tactile recognition we have discussed, we can soon find out what the problem might be. Very simply, some of the notes from the scale do not work against certain chords. If you play an E-7 and throw in an F note, there is a dissonant clash that in most contexts will not work harmonically. Similarly, with the C△7 (9,11,13) and A-7 (9, 11, b13) chord clusters from above, the F note in each case creates a problematic dissonance. The F note in all these cases, would be considered an "avoid" note. The good news in this caveat is that the modal cluster concept still applies, it is just a matter of being careful of which notes to avoid. In some cases, as in the D-7 (9,11,13), all the notes work. In other cases, it is usually a single note, and often the 4th note of the major scale source that creates the problematic dissonance. In a variety of potential scales and chords, along with the use of non-diatonic extensions, this issue of avoid notes will surface. With experience and an attentive ear, the avoid notes will become apparent. (Some of this will be addressed in Appendix 12 - Modal Chording, but you will primarily need to make these discoveries as you explore on your own. At least you have a good start recognizing the avoid note F in the major scale (the 4th note of the scale) as it is applied to certain chords. This is one of the most common avoid examples.)[78]

78. Try to take the time to understand the following - although complex, it will help to show the creative possibilities in this area of modes and chord coloring as well as being a great technical workout. Before proceeding, you should take to heart that the analysis below, although important, is another example of an after the fact construct. The point of this section on using modes within a diatonic system is to free up one's sense of harmony, not bog it down in analytical detail. For the evolved player, chord indications are merely a suggestion allowing for the taste and creativity of the player to fill in the space. Having said that, working through this technical understanding will help build your muscles and take you to that more intuitive place. Take your time ...

Here is a different way of looking at and identifying the chord with A in the bass and a white note cluster on top: I previously described this chord as an A-7 (9, 11, b13). Now, since F is generally an 'avoid' note on an A-7, we can try to visualize and hear the A root white note cluster chord as something other than an A-7. As I noted above, it's true that first we look at the root to identify a given chord, but there are also times when the bottom note might not be (or need to be) the root of a chord. An example of this would be an F chord voiced with A in the bass, followed in a higher range by the notes F and C. This is still an F chord – we covered this very important concept earlier in this study where a chord can be 'voiced' in any way on the keyboard. Keeping this in mind, within our A root note white note cluster chord, there is a triadic and seventh chord to identify other that the A-7. That chord is the F major triad. There is also an E note in the cluster, therefore, we can see that there is a F△7 chord in the A root note white note cluster chord! **A** (bottom note) B,**C**,D,**E**,**F**,G.

(Continued)

Ex. 10-8

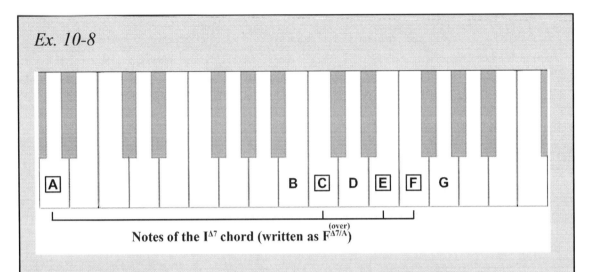

Notes of the I$^{\triangle 7}$ chord (written as F$^{\triangle 7/A}$ (over))

Now we are left only to identifying the other notes of this chord, the G, the B, and the D. These notes are the 9th (G), the sharp 11th (B), and the 13th (D) of the F chord. If we were to write this chord out, it might look something like this: F△7/A (9, #11, 13). (The sharp 11 note of this F major scale is derived by sharping the 11th note of the *F major scale* (Bb), to get the note B.)

Yes, this latter chord name is admittedly a bit of a mouthful! Here is another approach that might be easier and in some way more accurately describes the modal/cluster quality of this chord. Let's call it F Lydian/A. Does this make sense? A Lydian chord is formed by starting on the 4th note of the source C major scale – so here, we have that white note cluster conceptualized simply as an F Lydian scale with an A in the bass. This chord is fully diatonic, evokes a mode, and is a splendid sound as well.

MODES AND THE STANDARD JAZZ VOICINGS

A practical facility with the use of modes and clusters in the diatonic system should be grounded in a working understanding of the basic jazz voicings which have been outlined in the Standard Jazz Voicings Appendix. There is no short cut to this. If facility as a pianist is your goal, it will be important to spend time studying the appendix. For those who are not on a path to this type of pianistic facility, the example outlined below should provide enough material for a basic understanding of applying modes to diatonic chording. This material is also applicable for other instrumentalists or composers. In either case, we will be examining how a standard jazz voicing can provide the foundation to which modal color can be added or subtracted, or where notes can be reordered or reshaped.

To illustrate this, let's look at an example of how one simple standard voicing can be 'reshaped.' Assume we are working in the key of C major and we will use a V7 type chord (C7) to arrive to the IV chord of C which is F△7 (a I chord in relation to the C7 chord!). We then take the step to turn this V7 chord into a II V sequence to the F chord. This gives us G-7 to C7. Is this clear? Now, let's focus on the G-7 chord. The standard jazz voicing for this II-7 chord from the bottom up is FABbD (the 7th, 9th, 3rd and 5th).

Ex. 10-9

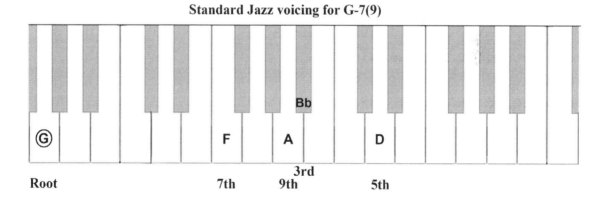

As we learned in the earlier chapter "INTRODUCING NON-DIATONIC NOTES AND 2 NEW SCALES," scale material for this G-7 is derived from the F major scale, therefore, the source material for applying modes will be F,G,A,Bb,C,D, and E.

Now, let's return to the standard jazz voicing which assumes the root G is being playing in the bass, and switch to our splashing color modal approach. We could remove notes from the voicing, and instead of playing FABbD we could use the 'cluster' ABbD or FABb. We could add notes to the voicing (two hands might be required) and get FABbD EFC, or take a piece of the left hand voicing and a splash with the right to get FABb CDG.

Ex. 10-10

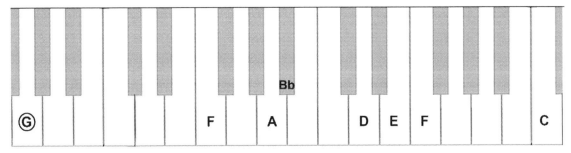

Standard Jazz voicing for $G^{-7(9)}$ with added "cluster" of notes

The possibilities are just about unlimited and we could then do the same thing for the V7 C7 chord that follows. Throw in some non-diatonic extension notes and we can really see how this modal palette, starting with the standard jazz voicings, can grow and be morphed into all kinds of shapes and colors. Please see Appendix 12 - Modes for additional examples of these possibilities.

A WORD ON CLUSTERS

As a final note on the topic of modes and their application to the diatonic system, you may have noticed how the notes of the chords outlined in Example 10-10 tend to be 'clustered,' in other words, they contain notes that are contiguous. Within the standard jazz voicing of G-7 9, the A is clustered with Bb. Those two notes played together present a fairly strong dissonance. However, with the addition of the D above, the F below, or both notes, the dissonance is lessened, and the chord can take on a more functional role leading to the C7. The somewhat passive, yet aesthetically pleasing color of this chord could also be used on its own outside the context of the II V sequence.

Ex. 10-11

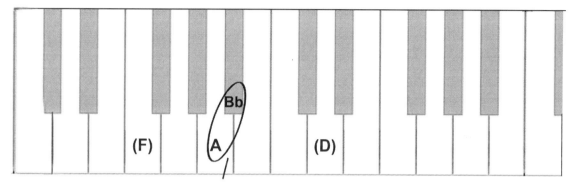

Dissonant cluster softened by adding F below and/or D above

Adding additional cluster notes within the G-7 chord can also serve to lessen the dissonance of the A and Bb played together. If one were to play the notes ABbC and D together, the sound is almost impressionistic, a sort of clouding of the edges as in the music of Debussy or Ravel, or in the paintings of Monet.

Ex. 10-12

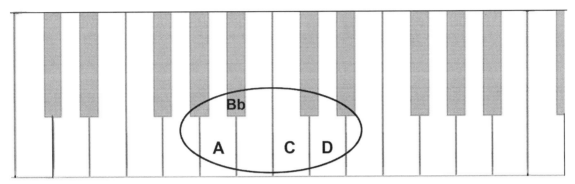

Impressionistic type chord using cluster from the F major scale

This use of clusters is common in jazz voicings and is one of the by-products of thinking modally when coloring diatonic chords (and diatonic chords with non-diatonic extensions). Bill Evans was an innovator and master of this style of chording. Keith Jarrett and Herbie Hancock have carried on this mantel. They are both masters at finding the balance between the passivity and impressionistic beauty of the clustered chords and adding just enough spice (often by way of non-diatonic extensions) to 'bite' deeper into the musical brain. Many of Keith Jarrett's introductory solos on his trio albums are great examples of this; the classic Miles Davis recordings of the early 60's, Four and More and My Funny Valentine, feature a young Herbie Hancock splashing modal color to great effect to produce probingly rich and complex chords that consistently maintain a unified logic. Take a look at this example of a chord typical of this style – an Ab△7, used here as the IV chord of the Eb major scale (Eb,F,G,Ab,Bb,C,D (Eb))

Ex. 10-13

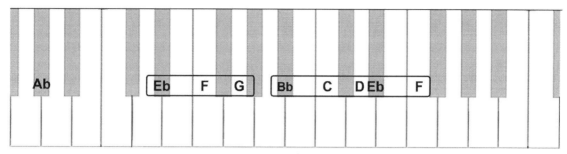

This cluster filled IV chord – Ab$^{\triangle 7}$ in the key of Eb – uses all of the notes of the Eb major scale (Eb, F, G, Ab, Bb, C, and D)

This chord contains the notes AbEbFG BbCDEbF. Notice that all the notes of the Eb chord are used to build this scale. While this may appear complex, it is formed simply by using a typical voicing of the Ab△7 chord - Ab (skip the C) Eb and G - and splashing modal color derived from the Eb major scale to fill out the sound.

On the other side of this filling out the chord idea, an aesthetic choice could be made to play a chord with minimal notes, perhaps one using a clustery sound (for example EbGAb to evoke Ab△7) or a more spread out chord using the notes Ab, the C an octave above, and G. It can be very effective at times to balance rich modal voicings with minimalism in the same way we looked at balancing diatonic with non-diatonic extensions, or dominant chords with sus chords, in order not to over-spice the musical dish.

Ex. 10-14

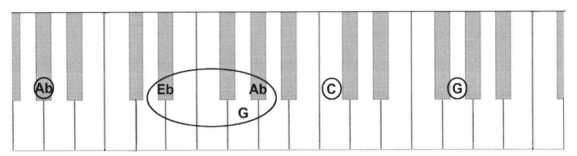

Two chord types: one clustered, the other more open and spread out

CHAPTER XI: OTHER EXPANDED APPROACHES

The diatonic system presented in this book covers much of Western harmony, however, it is not exhaustive of the subject. To reflect accurately how I approach harmony (and others as well), a few other topics need to be presented that, at least on their face, appear outside the diatonic system. These topics will also not be exhaustive of the possibilities within the realm of the non-diatonic, but they will at least cover some of the more common approaches.

The heading for these next sections could very well be "Because It Sounds Good," or perhaps, with a little tongue in cheek, "Not Everything Has To Be Explained!" However, as you may have anticipated, explain I will, at least those ideas that can be put into words. And there is a point to all this explaining – that is, to make harmony understandable from a broad perspective. There are dots that can be connected, and ultimately, we will find that these areas we perceive as falling outside the diatonic system most often remain connected in some way to an underlying diatonicism. In other words, it is somewhat rare for Western music to exist without some connection to the diatonic.

SYMMETRY AND SHAPE

By employing the ideas and the somewhat physical attributes of symmetry and shape, the diatonic boundaries of harmony can be expanded. The use of symmetry and shape is one of the most important tools in the creation of music, found in almost every facet of music. Rhythm, from classical symphonies to rock and roll is often constructed with repetitive patterns, symmetrical in shape. These rhythm patterns can be found within melodies as well as in accompaniment. In harmony, there are also countless uses of symmetry and shape. A chord sequence that repeats is a symmetrical shape. There is also symmetry between chords, for example, a minor seven chord moving to another minor seven chord. There can also be a sort of symmetry of movement when a non-diatonic extension note resolves a half step below and then that note continues to descend a half step into the note of the following chord. The half step movements are symmetrical shapes.

Ex. 11-1

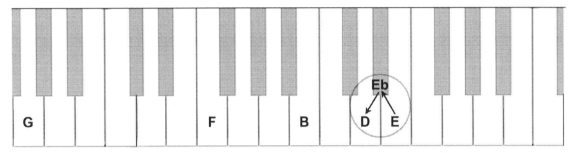

Descending symmetrical movement in half steps (G7 $^{13 \rightarrow b13 \rightarrow 5}$)

The musical effect of symmetry and shape in harmony is strong enough to exist on its own outside the diatonic system, although, as noted above, this is somewhat rare.[79] What is more often the case is that there will be elements within a diatonic piece of music that are best described with other means. Symmetry and shape is one of the most common of these elements.

> **79.** Ironicially, Arnold Schoenberg, to whom this books owes considerably for his insights on diatonic harmony developed the 12 tone system which completely abandoned diatonicism and instead used the 12 available notes, each one carrying its own weight. This music relied heavily on patterns and shapes to create a logic. "Twelve tone" music, although historically important and influential, remains somewhat of an intellectual connoisseur's art, rather than having had any staying power or in any way replacing the diatonic system that preceded its development. This further bears out the point that the non-diatonic aspects of music are most often built upon a diatonic foundation.

One example of symmetry and shape that falls outside the diatonic system, yet is still closely connected, is the quasi dominant movement of the half step. The G7 V chord going to the C△7 I chord can be substituted with a Db7 (the tritone substitution). We already looked at how notes within the Db7 chord including the root resolve by way of a half step movement. We also looked briefly at the following idea: *the movement in the root from Db to C is strong, so much so that the remainder of the Db chord does not need to be a dominant 7th chord.* In this way, instead of a typical type dominant to root chord resolution — **Db7** to C△7 — the sequence could move from **Db△7** to C△7.

Ex. 11-2

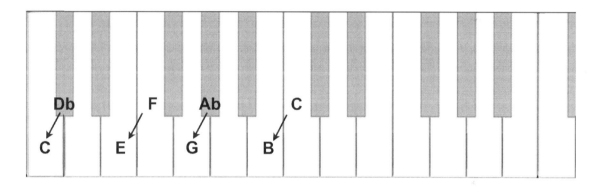

There are a few things going on in the above sequence, the first, already noted – the natural pull of the roots of the chords, Db to C. There is also a commonality of chords; both chords are major seven chords, and not only does *each* of the notes of the chords resolve a half step down, but the very fact that the chords are the same produces an intuitive harmonic logic. This is a wider phenomenon mentioned before - how moving between chords that are of the same character allows the ear to recognize something familiar. This idea can be used to great effect in different contexts. One example: in ending a jazz ballad, at times I might choose to move through a sequence of major seven chords. The effect can feel very much outside the key, but it maintains a logic because the ear is hearing the same chord type played in different 'keys'; the sound and shape of the chords produces a symmetry. This movement can be used with various chords, not just the major sevens.

To get a better sense of this idea, it might be helpful to imagine symmetry and shape in the visual world. In architecture and design, for example, it is common to see symmetrical shapes. The placement of windows in a building is usually ordered symmetrically, and not only for functional reasons. There are other repeating patterns within structures: doorways, balconies, and the like. Similarly, the color scheme of a structure will most often have an ordered design. In graphic art, the shape of text and the placement of photographs are carefully considered. Often, there will be some kind of symmetry at the core of this design. In a somewhat abstract visual artwork incorporating circles or squares in various sizes and colors, the effect is often achieved by the similarity of shape and/or the symmetry and placement of the shapes. A cascading sequence might be used or a sequence of similar shapes diminishing or increasing in size.

Music can incorporate these same types of patterns and sequences. Gradual movement from loud to soft is like the diminishing size of a common shape. The eye (or ear) becomes used to what will happen next – there is a logic. In the example of the major seven chords I presented, in addition to the commonality of the chords, the shape of the chord movement can be used to create logic. If I were to descend from C△7 to A△7 to F△7 to D△7 to Bb△7 to A△7, the continued movement downward sets up a logic that is heightened by the use of the same chord type. The beauty of a sequence like this is that, while there is something relatable in the sequence, there is also a sense of traveling far from the sometimes too unsurprising and familiar world of the diatonic.

<u>Symmetry and shape does not necessarily apply only to chord sequences; it can be used to build the chords themselves</u>. One example of this type of

chord is one built on the fourth interval. A C chord constructed this way could be voiced with C in the root followed by EADG.

Ex. 11-3

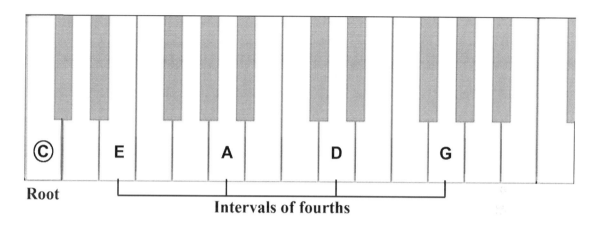

This chord happens to be diatonic in the key of C (a C 6,9 chord). If a chord was voiced completely in fourths, for example starting on F, it would consist of the notes F and BbEbAbDb, clearly a non-diatonic chord in relation to the key of C.

Ex. 11-4

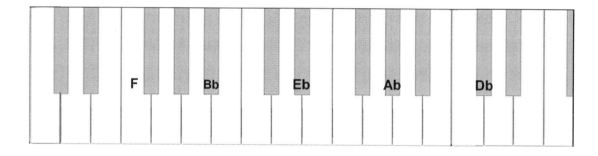

McCoy Tyner, most famous for his work with John Coltrane developed a style in large part based on the use of this type of chord. Instead of assuming to play diatonic chords and related dominants and quasi-dominants, he often used the fourth chord to create a forceful geometric sound shape, at once abstract yet somehow entirely logical. The consistent shape of the fourths

> **80.** Two points: first, McCoy Tyner's work, even with the heavy use of the often non-diatonic fourths chords, is often overlayed on a diatonic piece of music. The power and tension created through the non-diatonicism of the fourths is made possible, at least in part, because of an underlying sense of a diatonic system that is serving to root his explorations. Second, on a purely aesthetic note: listen to McCoy Tyner's work on John Coltrane's classic recording "My Favorite Things." This not only is a great example of McCoy Tyner's fourths style of playing, but John Coltrane's joyful and soulful explorations are a musical treasure to behold. This recording was one of the main gates I entered to witness the world of jazz with new eyes.

within this chord drives the inner logic of his style.[80]

The fourth chord used in sequence is perhaps one of the strongest examples of a sound that can skirt the outside of the diatonic realm. Other chords of atypical shape and source can also be used this way, from something very simple like a clustery type voicing on a minor 7 chord, to a strangely shaped chord of seeming illogic.

Ex. 11-5

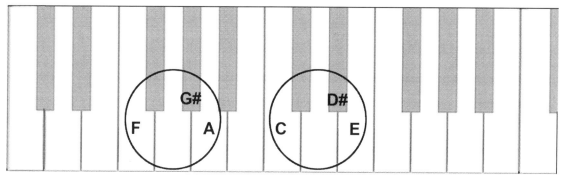

The Sequencing of two symmetrical harmonic shapes,
however dissonant, can create its own logic

By repeating these same chord types starting on different roots, either in ascending or descending movement, or even random movement, the ear will identify with the repeated intervallic relationship of the notes within the chord. It may even be that the more bizarre the chord, the more the ear will recognize when that chord is repeated. This concept allows for a considerable amount of harmonic freedom and room to roam outside the diatonic system, but, of course, as with all liberties, it must be handled with care.[81]

> **81.** Melodic phrases can be used to the same effect. Beethoven was well-known for the use of these repetitive 'motifs,' his most famous being the opening and development of the first movement of the Fifth Symphony. John Coltrane was also very much into the use of motifs played in different keys, in and outside a diatonic system. Two examples of this can be found in his pieces "A Love Supreme" and "Giant Steps." Interestingly, it would seem that Coltrane's non-diatonic explorations must have had some kind of influence in driving McCoy Tyner's harmonic innovations.

Western Harmony Simplified

II V MOVEMENT, MODULATIONS, AND NEO-SOUL

The II V progression is a chord sequence we have covered as it applies to the diatonic system. We have also seen that the II V can be a substitution for a non-diatonic dominant chord being used to change keys. (Remember the example of a C7 V chord changed to a G-7 C7 (a II V) that leads to the F chord which could either be the IV chord of the C diatonic system, or the I chord of the new key F). II V progressions can also be used to indicate a new key, but not necessarily resolve to that key. An example: a somewhat common jazz influenced progression is a C chord followed by a F-7 to Bb7 and returning to the C chord. The F-7 to Bb7 can be seen as a II V in the key of Eb, but being left unresolved (to Eb), we are left to explain how this progression seems to work so well as two non-diatonic chords played within C major.

The explanation might not be completely satisfying with regard to non-diatonicism. Before diving in, I'm also reminded of my admonition early in this chapter that "not everything has to be explained!" However, as it turns out, this seeming non-diatonic progression of chords can be explained within the diatonic system, and in doing so, we can see further the extent of connections that can be made within this system. First, let's look at the Bb7 chord as it 'resolves' to the C chord. We can see that, as voiced below, the Ab and F of the Bb7 chord resolve in half steps to the G and E of the C chord.

Ex. 11-6

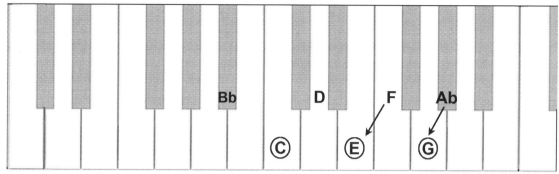

**Half step resolutions from
Bb⁷ chord to C**

This is very similar to how the B and F of the G7 V chord resolve to the C and E of the C chord. Essentially, in this way, the Bb7 can be viewed as a dominant type chord leading to the C. Looking at a variation of the progression, what if we were to use C followed by **F-7 only** (no Bb chord) and back to C. We could do the same type of analysis and notice that the Ab and Eb of the F-7 chord resolve by half steps to the G and E of the C chord. The F note of the F-7 chord could also resolve a half step down to E. This use of half step resolution used creatively can open up all kinds of possibilities of approaches to chord movement.[82]

> **82.** There is also a bottom line that this progression just happens to sound good – something in the switch from major to minor between the triads (symmetry and shape?!). Also note, there is a practical reason for stating, "not everything has to be explained": heaven forbid that one's creative explorations be inhibited by the need for theoretical justification for every harmonic choice. Mistakes can be wonderful and whatever the ear finds intriguing should be enthusiastically examined!

Ex. 11-7

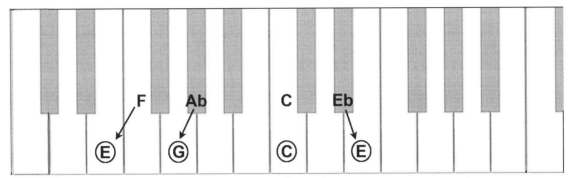

Half step resolutions from F-⁷ chord to C

Another powerful effect of the half step, which we have covered to some extent in another context, is using this interval to modulate temporarily from a given diatonic key. When a Db△7 chord is played which then moves to C△7, the Db△7 can be seen as a chord which in passing resolves to C△7, serving essentially as a dominant type chord. It can also be seen as a temporary modulation to the key of Db. In an improvisational setting, it is possible for a player to be in the key of C and, instead of playing C, to play in the key of Db for some time. If this is a piano player, the bass player may follow or not; either way, the effect will be one of tension and at the same time a feeling of temporarily switching keys. Playing in Db while the piece is calling for C is about as non-diatonic as can be, however, it also shows that the 'correct' note is merely a half step away. Perhaps one could say that this feeling of being a half step away from a 'correct' note (or chord) is what allows playing a half step away to feel somehow appropriate.

This concept can be expanded even further – why not play an additional half step away from the half step away, that is, extrapolate the expanded harmony to D which can then 'resolve' to Db which in turn resolves to the home key C. Yes, a bit complex, but it can get even go deeper. The idea of extending half steps away can also incorporate the diatonic chord types and sequences

156   Western Harmony Simplified

we have covered – the V to Vs, tritone substitutions, sus chords, and the like. The possibilities are great, but in other ways limited; the harmonic extrapolations seem to be most effective when the thread to the original diatonic is not broken.

Focusing more specifically on modulation, the feeling of being outside the key does not have to be temporary. Modulation is a very effective tool to expand the scope of a melody, and to provide a musical change of scenery. The classical composers modulated through keys for their musical pleasure; the study of their varied means is beyond the scope of this book, but we have already covered some of the basics. We saw this clearly in the dominant chord with non-diatonic tone(s) leading to the new key (i.e., C7 to F). Many songs, particularly from the Broadway, popular music, and jazz standards repertoire are prone to modulate, particularly at the bridge (the mid-section release before returning to the main melody). An example of this is in the popular American standard "The Way You Look Tonight" which modulates from the key of F to Ab in the bridge. At this point, the player will at least temporarily be 'thinking' in the new key of Ab; the diatonic scale system of Ab will then define the chords and melodies for that section. Modulation can also be used effectively to increase the excitement of a repeated section of music. Stevie Wonder used this Gospel based idea effectively at the end of his song "Golden Lady." In all these examples, the modulations do not represent a move into the non-diatonic realm as much as a switch to a new diatonic key.

Finally, having had the opportunity to immerse myself in the style of "Neo-Soul," a jazz and underground influenced type of R&B, I've made some harmonic discoveries relevant to this genre that at least point towards non-diatonicism. It seems that some of the songs from this style are coming out of a 'non-schooled' musical mentality. The bass lines sometimes do not quite match the chords which within themselves are at times difficult to pin down. In my own compositional work in this area, I've found that plugging in a chord not relevant in any diatonic way to the sequence, or a II V that leads nowhere, or a minor chord where one would expect a major, leads to some intriguing yet logical results. My temptation is to pass this logic off as "not everything needs to be explained," or that "it just sounds good," but my sense is that there are a few explainable elements here. First, as we keep seeing, all notes and many chords are at most only a half step away from a resolving note or chord. This may seem to be a bit of a cop-out coverall, but the appearance of a pat answer doesn't obscure the reality of this physics of sound. Second, switches from major to minor and movement between minor chords both fall within the realm and logic of symmetry and shape. Finally, as we have already seen, repeated sequential movement is another form of symmetry and shape. Expanding on this idea, if a seeming illogical chord sequence is repeated, the logic can begin to emerge. In a twisted sort of way, the logic is built on its illogic. But here, lest illogic try to claim dominance over logic, it should be remembered that there would be no context for the unorthodox idea without the preexistence of a more familiar resolution.

FOLK CHORDING

We have looked at harmony mainly from the perspective of the classical and jazz traditions. We have also looked at modes or at least certain applications of modes which tend to take us out of these traditions, but this has been the exception. The thrust of this presentation has been the analysis of diatonic chords derived from the major and minor scales and the important role of the dominant or 'quasi-dominant' chord – the core of classical and jazz harmony. Throughout this analysis it is inevitable to miss some styles in between these traditions. While these styles are still grounded in the diatonic system and, in fact, would not exist, but for the classical and/or jazz traditions, they can offer a different angle by which to view the diatonic elements. One such style is one I call "folk chording." We will take a closer look at this approach but first, a little more on what my use of the term folk is referring to. The generic term folk music refers to music derived from people of a community (e.g., Appalachia, the English countryside...) that most often is passed on by way of an oral tradition; it is not 'art' music, and is at times simpler in approach than music coming out of the classical or jazz traditions. Of course, one needs to be careful with this latter point because there are various styles of folk music that reveal an incredible sophistication, whether it be the breakneck speed and accuracy of America bluegrass or the complex rhythms of Afro-Cuban music. In any event, our discussion of folk music refers mostly to the guitar based American folk and rock styles, as developed by the likes of Woodie Guthrie, Bob Dylan, Joni Mitchell, James Taylor, Neil Young, and yes, even rock acts, like the Rolling Stones.

The connection to be made between folk music and the diatonic system lies in folk music's ability to be within the diatonic system and yet also remain aloof. What I call "folk chording" is essentially a way of playing through a diatonic system using the diatonic chords themselves, modally based chords and scales, and generally, fewer dominant chords moving to resolution chords. It is this use of fewer dominants, the not being so bound to the requirements and tendencies of these chords that gives folk music its wings. Certainly, it doesn't hurt that folk music is often telling a story through words and therefore doesn't require complex harmonic movement. In any regard, with or without words, there is a delight in playing chords with a folk emphasis. To be sure, resonating with this style requires an ability to hear a joyful simplicity in a few chords, but this connection can be utilized to inform more complex genres. Keith Jarrett, Pat Metheny, and Joni Mitchell are just a few of the artists who have integrated folk music into their sound and style, evolving yet remaining true to the folk element.

My personal approach to folk chording involves both the chord sequences and the chords themselves. As described above, the chord sequences in the folk style can often be quite simple. Using the C major diatonic system, a common folk and rock progression is a G triad to an F triad to a C triad. Leonard Skynard's "Sweet Home Alabama" uses this progression in the key of D, as does James Taylor's "Country Road." The Rolling Stones' "Sympathy for the Devil" employs this sequence starting on the E triad. Another example of a commonly used folk like sequence is a movement between the

I and IV chord, finally punctuated with a V chord / C / F / C / F / C / F / G / G /. The importance of these sequence types, of which there are many, is their tendency to bring you into a world of sound that can provide a ready made canvas for expression as we saw with the 'blues.' Within this canvas, the chords can be kept simple and triadic, a sound that can be the most appropriate for the context, as well as starkly beautiful. This canvas is also very receptive to the more clustery modal approach we looked at previously.

Let's take a closer look at this modal approach using the "Country Road" chords, D, C and G. First, perhaps there is a budding harmony detective among you readers who noticed there is something a bit odd with my reference to this progression as being in "D"...? The oddity lies in the fact that there is no C chord in a D major scale, or at least there is no diatonic C chord in the key of D.

Ex. 11-8

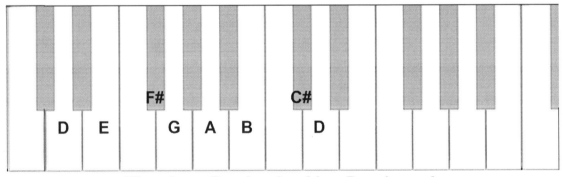

There is no C major chord in a D major scale

The answer to this puzzle is that the progression in D major is built from the G major scale. Here, D is the root note, the home note of the key using a Mixolydian scale. (The Mixolydian scale is derived from the major scale starting a fifth below). Within this modal scale, the chords D, C and G major are diatonic.

Ex. 11-9

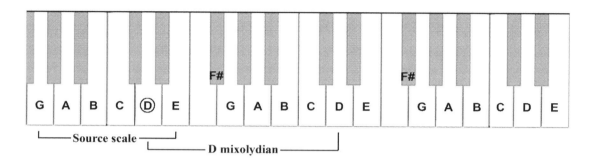

Now that we have this mini-review out of the way, we can look at the types of chords that can populate this progression. Again, we could play the chords simply and triadically. The choices will depend on the context. My approach would generally incorporate the modal, likely blending a respect for the power of the triad and the 'feel' of the progression with other elements to blur the edges.

Ex. 11-10

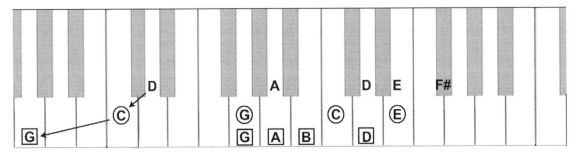

D to C to G progression using folk modal chording

In this example, we can see the modal approach, but what makes this work in real life is a sensitivity to the sound of the notes and clusters within the progression. The more this sensitivity is developed, the more it can be incorporated into chord progressions from other styles and help to keep you in the moment of the sound. This awareness is something that can get lost as the harmony becomes more complex. Alas, the folk approach to harmony can be a great teacher!

DIMINISHED AND AUGMENTED CHORDS – "the vagrant chords"

The Diminished Chord

In our examination of the diatonic chords, we saw that the VII chord in the key of C major is a B diminished chord containing the notes B, D, and F. As a four note diatonic seventh chord, the chord becomes a B half diminished. It is considered a half diminished chord because the interval between the F and A notes is a major third, not the minor third by which a full diminished is formed. One of the functions of this half diminished seventh chord is to serve as the II chord in the relative minor key to C major: A minor. This is one of the most common uses of this diminished chord as an independent chord.

Ex. 11-11

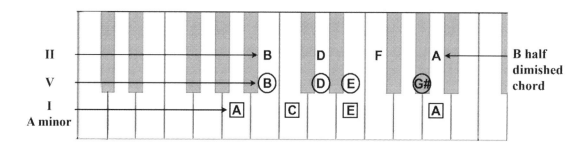

The half diminished chord, commonly referred to as a minor seven flat 5 chord, also does extensive service as a discretionary chord. Just as a player or composer has the discretion to turn a II chord into a dominant chord, taste may dictate turning the II chord of a major diatonic system into this minor seven flat 5 chord. The first three chords of the Cole Porter standard "Night and Day," as played by many jazz musicians, are D-7 b5 to G7 to C△7. The Ab of the D-7 b5 chord is not diatonic, but it happens to have an appealing sound and gives this song a different flavor. This idea of using the minor 7 flat 5 in place of the diatonic II chord can be carried out any time a player sees a II V I major progression. Here is yet another opportunity for discretion, and hopefully, a discretion that will not be overused.

Within the C major diatonic system, the B diminished and B half diminished seventh chords serve primarily as the upper structure of the V7 G7 chord. The notes of the B diminished chord – B, D, and F – are the 3rd, 5th and 7th notes of the G7 chord. The notes of the B diminished half seven chord – B, D, F, and A – are the 3rd, 5th 7th, and 9th notes of the G7 chord.

Western Harmony Simplified

Ex. 11-12

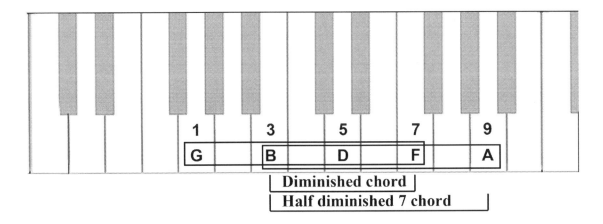

Because these diminished chords are essentially the same chord as the V chord (minus the root), there was not much to add about this VII chord as we initially discussed the chords of the diatonic system. The functional implications of the VII chord were covered in our discussion of the V chord.

There is a distinctly important function of the diminished chord as formulated within the classical tradition that is worth noting (also applying to the augmented chord which will be examined in more detail below). Due to its symmetrical make-up, a full diminished chord – a four note chord made up entirely of minor thirds, i.e., BDFAb – can function in a variety of ways as a V7 chord. In our diatonic key of C, the BDFAb diminished chord sounds as the 3rd, 5th, 7th, and flat 9th of the V7 G7 chord and functions well in this capacity. Amazingly enough, with or without moving notes around (using a different inversion), this same chord can function as three other V7 chords: Bb7 (a V chord in the key of Eb), Db7 (a V chord in the key of Gb), and E7 (a V chord in the key of A).

Ex. 11-13

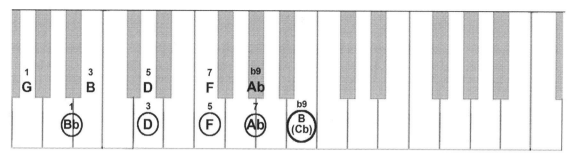

The full diminished chord BDFAb can serve as the 3, 5, 7, and b9 of four dominant chords. Above are the examples of G⁷ and Bb⁷.

Because of this ability of the full diminished chord to 'morph' into four different V7 chords, it has a very flexible capacity to connect one key to another. Imagine that you are in the key of C and play this diminished chord BDFAb. This could be used as the literal V chord (G7 b9) to return to the I chord, but also, in the proper context, this chord could be used to modulate from the key of C to the key of Gb. This Gb key is as far away from the key of C as one could imagine, yet, it is possible by way of this diminished chord to make the connection. That's a chord with a lot of talent![83]

---

83. Two additional points regarding the diminished chord: 1) Because of the diminished chord's dissonance and restless quality, it was sometimes used in classical music, not only as a transition chord, but as a stressed chord to indicate an emotional tension. Nowadays we know this sound as the cliché movie chord that sounds absolutely old fashioned. The augmented chord was used to similar effect. 2) There are three diminished chords and accompanying scales – for a more advanced review, please see Appendix 13 - Diminished and Augmented Chords.

Ex. 11-14

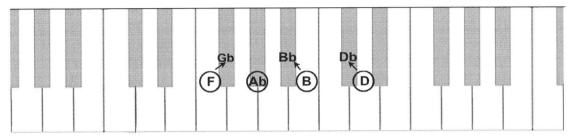

This full diminished chord facilitates a smooth modulation to Gb

The Augmented Chord

The augmented chord, a non-diatonic chord as applied to the major diatonic system, is formed by sharping (or 'augmenting') the 5th note of a major triad. A C augmented chord, also written as C+, contains the notes C, E, and G#; An F+ chord contains the notes F, A, and C#.

The augmented chord shares traits with the diminished chord. In fact, Arnold Schoenberg referred to both these chords as "vagrant" chords for their shared traits. Both chords are symmetrical in their intervallic formation (the diminished chord is built on consecutive minor thirds while the augmented chord is built on major third intervals). Due to this formation, the root of both these chords is hard to define, therefore, giving the chords an ambiguous quality that allows them to slip in between more defined chords.

Ex. 11-15

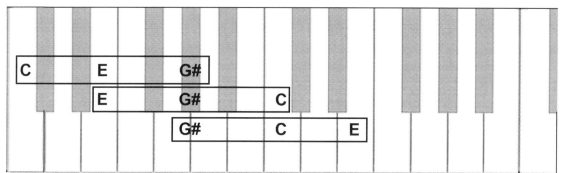

The notes C, E and G# in their 3 configurations form the C,E and G# augmented chord

Examining the effect of this ambiguity more closely, the augmented chord, like the diminished chord, is a chord that can create a bridge towards resolution if not outright modulation. Within itself, the augmented fifth – the G# in the C augmented chord - is drawn towards the natural 5th. This G# to G movement is no different from the numerous examples we have looked at of a half step creating the need for resolution. In the same C+ chord, the G# could also resolve to the A note (half steps also can be drawn upwards) resulting in either a C6 chord or an A minor chord in the first inversion.

Ex. 11-16

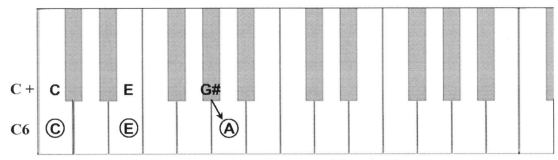

C augmented resolution to C6 or A minor

This latter resolution to A minor shows the inherent flexibility of the augmented chord. The C+ chord could also be read as an E+ chord (the same chord starting on a different note) in order to effectuate a smooth sounding transition to the A minor chord.

Ex. 11-17

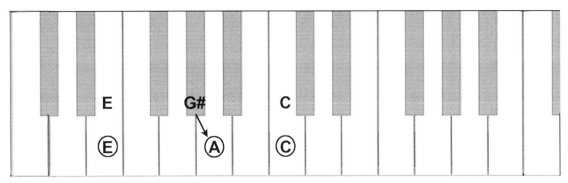

E + resolution to A minor

Carrying this notion further, like the diminished chord, the augmented chord can promote the connection of seemingly disconnected keys; in other words, it can create radical modulation. Let's trace how this can happen starting with the chord we initially identified as C augmented. First step: recognize that the C+ chord can also be identified as an E+ or G# + (a.k.a. Ab+). Second step: understand that we can use these three augmented chords as a V type chord to modulate to the key of F, A, or Db respectively, and for now, choose to modulate to the key of Db, because it happens to be the 'furthest' – the key with the least amount of common notes – from the key of C.[84] Final step: choose a voicing that promotes a smooth transition between the Ab+ chord and the Db resolution chord.

> **84.** The augmented chord serving as the V chord can resolve to either a major or minor key.

Ex. 11-18

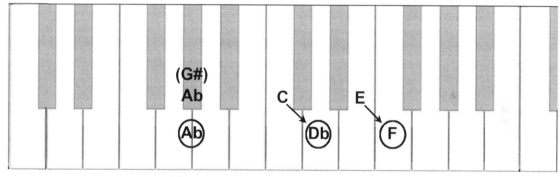

Ab augmented resolved to Db

If you play the above chord sequence, you might notice that the effect of the augmented to the resolution chord is very similar to the effect derived from a V7 chord with non-diatonic extension notes moving to its resolution chord. In the illustration below (in the key of C for simplification), you can see that the only difference in the 'V' chords is that the official 'seventh' chord contains the seventh note. The effect is practically the same – play through the two set-up chords to see how close these progressions are. Having noted this sameness and now moving towards a more subtle level, you might notice a degree of richness in the V7 chord compared with the leanness of the augmented chord. The choice between these two set-up chords can make a difference and help to define one's style and approach.

Ex. 11-19

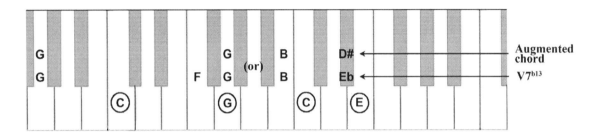

POLYCHORDS AND PEDAL POINTS

Polychords and pedal points are two tools which can be used to stretch harmony towards its outer barriers. The rewards of this exploration can be a mining of the mysterious, the realms of harmony that evoke something potentially new, but still strangely familiar - recognizable. *Polychords* are formed by the juxtaposition of two chords, often triads or seventh chords. *Pedal points* are formed by the juxtaposition of a repeated or sustained single note[85] either in the bass or in a higher range against a movement of chords. Although both these techniques can be considered to 'stretch' the outer boundaries of the harmonic system, the techniques can also be 'explained' comfortably within the systems presented in this book. The main thesis – that of a strong foundational diatonic system of chords expanded by dominant or domi-

> **85.** It is possible for the pedal tone to be more than one note, as in an interval of a fifth, an octave, or some other group of notes. The defining characteristic of the pedal tone is its singularity of sound.

nant type chords - applies in both instances, as does the concept of symmetry and shape.

Polychords

In the example below, a polychord is formed by playing an E- chord over a D-7. The result is a darkly sensual chord, one that is at bit impressionistic, modal and harmonically unified. This 'unity' has a clear explanation: the notes of the chord E- over D-7 are completely diatonic within the key of C. This chord can also be written as a D-7 (9,11,13).[86]

> **86. The use of the notes of the C major scale to form this D-7 chord evokes the D Dorian mode.**

Ex. 11-20

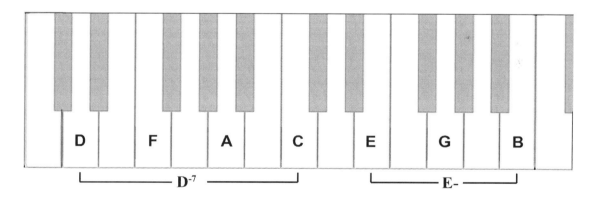

The above example once again shows the importance of becoming familiar with the scale of the diatonic system. As in the modal approach to chording, with polychords, one can with a bit of abandon (tempered by experience and trial and error) simply play two chords on top of each other using the notes of the diatonic scale. This may be an easier way to form a complex chord involving extensions rather than thinking of and forming a chord from bottom to top with a burdened sense of the numerical degrees of the scale.

Here, you might be justified in thinking that the above does not present a real 'stretch' of the harmonic system as promised, after all, the resulting chord was diatonic, one which we have already covered. Well, that was just a warm-up - here goes: instead of placing an E minor chord on top of the D-7, let's put an Eb triad over a pure D sus chord.

Ex. 11-21

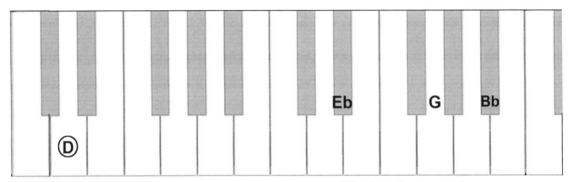

Eb chord over D bass

The resulting chord is quite dissonant, but, for my ears, not so much so that the chord falls out of the realm of any context. Here, the context is D minor, and within the D minor tonality, the polychord creates a jaggedness and a tension that calls for a resolution. Not surprisingly, the theoretical underpinnings of this relationship bear out my aural characterization. The Eb triad contains the notes Eb G, and Bb. The G is already diatonic so we needn't worry about resolving that note, or, alternatively, that voice can move to the F to create a resolution towards a D minor chord. The Eb and Bb notes are resolvable within the half step (as is any note in this system!!). These notes pull toward the diatonic notes of E and B, or D and A respectively.

Ex. 11-22

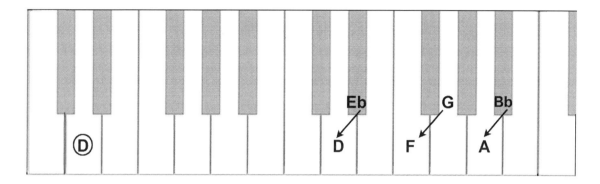

Again, we have that seemingly pat answer - resolution is only a half step away in any instance. Yes, this is true and happens to be one of if not the most important concepts presented within this harmonic system. The simplicity of the system does not devalue its worth, and I am sure you must have recognized by now that within this 'simplicity,' there is plenty to work with!

Finally, the polychord approach to building chords can be particularly useful in the formation of chords with non-diatonic extensions. Taking the chord C△7 and placing a D triad on top forms the chord containing the notes C, E, G, B and D, F#, and A.

Ex. 11-23

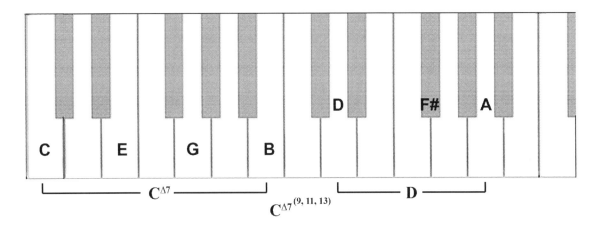

One could visualize this chord as a C△7 with a D triad on top or merely see the chord C△7 with the extensions within the scale. Either way, the resulting chord is C△7 (9 #11, 13). Again, here we can see how a polychord forms a diatonic chord with extension notes that are both diatonic (the 9th and the 13th) and non-diatonic (the 11th).[87] Another example follows below of a polychord built on the G7 V chord. This chords contains two non-diatonic extension notes.

> **87.** In the D triad over C△7, there is also a noteworthy **symmetry and shape**. In addition to having the same structural formation, the C and D triads of this polychord 'ring' as major triads. Although the chord has an integrated sound, the individual chords seep through. The ear on some level is likely recognizing these simultaneous major shapes.

Ex. 11-24

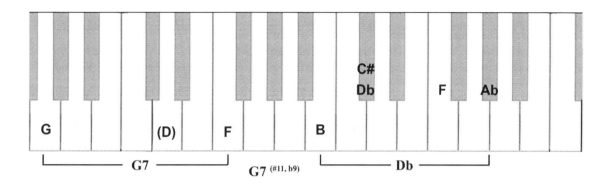

Pedal Points

Pedal points are an easy study applied to dominant tonic resolutions and symmetry and shape. Pedal points by definition establish a center which all other material orbits around. There is a natural pull towards this center, an inherent tension release serviced by dominant, and even dominant to dominant to tonic resolutions. There is also symmetry and shape in this natural gravitational movement of orbital bodies towards a center.

Bringing these spatial notions down to the more earthbound locale of musical notes, let's examine the opening chords of the American standard "Green Dolphin Street." These opening chords are: C△7, Eb/C, D/C, Db/C, C△7.[88] In this case, the C bass tone is the pedal note, and the individual chords are the harmony orbiting around this center. The downward chromatic movement of this progression is a 'shape' symmetrical in its descent by equal half

> **88.** An Eb chord with C in the bass is written as Eb/C and would be called an Eb over C. The same is true for any chord intended over the C bass. A D chord over C is written as D/C; the D to the left of the slash refers to the chord, and the C to the right of the slash refers to the bass note. This is common notation.

Western Harmony Simplified

steps. There is also a symmetry and shape in the use of the same chord type as the harmony descends. Like this abstract picture of a circle in descent, the downward movement of the chords creates its own form of aural descent.

Ex. 11-25

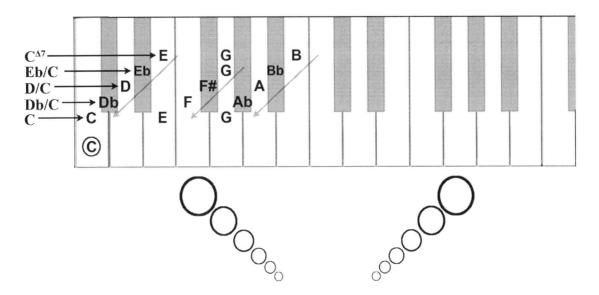

It is also instructive to note that the Eb over C (Eb/C) can be read as a C-7 (the notes are the same in each chord: CEbGBb). Further indicating the power of this idea of symmetry and shape, within the context of the chord sequence, the ear tends to hear the notes C, Eb, G and Bb as an Eb triad over C rather than as a C-7. As the chord moves from Eb major to D major to Db major over the C pedal note, the ear becomes accustomed to this shape of chord and its directional movement and identifies the Eb as a triad along with the other major triads D and Db.

The dominant to tonic relationships in the "Green Dolphin Street" progression are also quite evident. The movement from one major triad to the next a half step below exemplifies the half step dominant tonic relationship which keeps surfacing in this study. The Eb moves to D which then moves to Db which resolves finally to C. Each of these movements is powered by the half step relationships. For example, the Eb triad serves as a dominant type chord to D which then serves as a dominant type chord to Db and so forth. There is an additional element of magnetism in this progression. Because of the C pedal in the bass, as each chord is moving towards the chord a half step below forming a dominant tonic relationship, there is also an even stronger magnetism of the whole progression moving towards the C.

The above exemplifies one of the main functions and effect of the pedal point in that it creates an anchor, one with enough power not only to draw chords to it but to allow a freedom for chords to roam about without getting too lost in harmonic ambiguity. By laying down a C bass, there is a flexibility of what can be played on top. In a sense, this pedal point can be considered the root of a dynamic mode, one that can change from major to minor, from one mode to another, and also serve as the root for a string of seemingly disparate chords.[89]

---

89. There are two additional points worth noting on this topic. First: in the "Green Dolphin Street" progression, discretionary dominant sevenths could be used in place of the major triads. This discretionary use is always contextual- in this instance, each of these triads is serving as a dominant type chord to the next, so there is no reason other than melodic considerations to not go all the way and turn these chords into full dominant seventh chords. The overall sound of course would change – the harmony turning a bit bluesier, and therefore affecting the choices in the improvisations. Second: pedal points can be used in the higher range as in a sustained string note or some form of ostinato (a repetitive rhythmic figure) played by a keyboard or guitar. Although these pedal points in the higher range generally do not have the harmonic power and magnetism of the bass pedal points, they do serve as anchors and can be effective in a variety of contexts.

CHAPTER XII: SOME CLOSING THOUGHTS

As I have presented this material, I've heard a quiet inner voice repeating, "It's even simpler than this." On the other hand, what could be more simple? In Western music, there are twelve available tones organized into scales of seven notes, major or minor. The remaining five notes are very close neighbors that allow for a temporary or permanent move away from the seven note scale. The mechanics of this seven note scale and the seven chords that can be formed within it are 100 percent applicable to each of the twelve scales. Yet, perhaps it could even be simpler – because the diminished VII chord is essentially an extension of the V7 chord, we could say that there are only six basic chords within the system. Perhaps this can be reduced further down to a few chords! A C△7 (9) has the chord E-7 (minus the C bass) within it; an E minor 7 chord has a G major chord within it; a C chord is the upper structure of an A-7; the G7 chord contains B diminished - you get the idea. Along with the limited number of notes in the scale, recognizing the connections and overlap between the diatonic chords can go a long way towards streamlining the learning process.

My intent in writing this book has been to present a system of harmony stripped down to its essentials. Hopefully, you now have a clearer understanding of the diatonic elements and how they function together as a whole – keeping it all simple! For those of you who may have been looking for something more complex, consider again the case of Arnold Schoenberg, whose understanding of the evolution of harmony has deeply influenced my own harmonic awareness and practice. As a composer, Schoenberg sought out ways to break free of the structure and tonal qualities of the diatonic system. He came up with the twelve tone system which seemingly had no relationship to the diatonic system that had been the engine of classical composition for centuries. The resulting compositions were influential for a time in the world of the modern 20th century composer, but this influence was short-lived, certainly when compared to the staying power of Western diatonic harmony. The bottom line is that sound organic to the ear, even when it is unpredictable, is what the ear wants to hear. The diatonic system is something inherent in nature: the relationship of the notes of the scale to each other by way of the overtone series; the natural pull within the half step intervals; the home feeling of the octave throughout the frequency ranges; the power of the major and minor chords; and, the incredible array of chords and colors and melodies that somehow speak of familiar things.

Beyond all these explanations, justifications, and theoretical proofs, there lies the at times indescribable musical power – the ability of music to evoke the widest range of emotions and feeling, from ecstatic joy and hope to terrible sadness, from the purely sensual to the higher aspirations of the human spirit, from a familiar sense of home to a journey leading to the unknown. All of this is made possible through the fundamental diatonic structure presented here. To be sure, there are other systems of harmony, even those using scales different than our own, as in Indian, Arabic, and Javanese music, and there is nothing holding us back from incorporating these musical worlds into our own, both as performers, and as listeners. For the most part, however, in the 'western' world, we are steeped in the music built on the system described throughout this book.

Music, of course, is about something beyond the theoretical, even if this theory provides a comprehensive outline and tools for moving into the ineffable, those regions which resist explanation. It is this attachment to the indefinable worlds that can best drive the harmonic search, or even the simplest application of harmony through repetitive rhythmic pulse.

There is also Charles Ives, whose idea of a musical good time was the sound of two parade bands marching towards each other and the resulting cacophony. There is Edgard Varese whose distillation of real world sounds into musical composition ("musique concrete") created some quite interesting and at times entertaining results, and whose music has arguably been an important influence on composers in disparate genres from rap/sampling to film scores. There is John Cage, whose piece 4'33" is nothing but silence for the length of time indicated in the title. Ultimately, music is yin and yang – the juxtaposition of opposites: sound on / sound off, loud / soft, bright / dark, cold / hot, joy / pain . . . One could argue that the expression of this yin and yang can be in whatever form a creator chooses.

Certainly, there have been and will be contemporary explorations that fall outside the diatonic system and manage to engage the listener's spirit as well as intellect. I would contend they do so because the listener understands that he or she can always return home, that there is some kind of reference point. Whether this be in the use of micro-tonal scales or those musics that reside deep within the non-diatonic, much of the tension and emotion is based on the listener's sense of distance away from the familiar. Perhaps this distance from the diatonic can be seen as a form of suspended dominant, or a dominant tonic relationship of a different degree.

Music, in the final analysis, is an experience for the ears, brain and spirit of the listener, whether this listener be passive or the actual creator of the sound. Much of the theoretical explorations testing the flexibility of the definition of music may only be (and have been) wishful thinking. For the reality appears to be that the diatonic system, at least for our Western ears, has steadfastly provided and will continue to provide the material or at least a reference point for conveying the language of music. Perhaps in the future, there will be discovered some form of sound based on the mechanics of frequencies, something we haven't heard yet that will ring true to our souls. It is also my contention that, in some ways, the more we have sought out this new sound without a connection to the organic, the more distant we have become from our natural expression. Now, through technological development, the entry into the digital world and the ability to access countless 'newer and newer' sounds, it seems at times that our connection with the power of music has only diminished. This is why 'retro' often sounds new, and the modern often has struck us as cold and aloof, but this is a topic for another book. In the meantime, we are stuck here on earth, with our mere twelve tones and seven note scales; there is plenty to be mined within this seeming simplicity.

Appendices

Staff Notation for the Non-Reader

Many of the examples in the appendices will be using staff notation. This notation will be laid out clearly enough for those with little or no experience reading music. If you are one of these people, take a look at these examples and explanations before moving into the main appendix sections.

Music is written on a two "staff" system. The middle C of the keyboard is written in between the two staffs. Notes above middle C are the notes sounding higher and notes written below middle C sound lower.

Notes sounding above middle C of the keyboard are generally written in the treble (aka "G") clef.

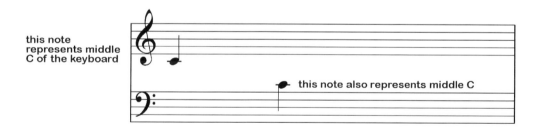

this note represents middle C of the keyboard

this note also represents middle C

Notes sounding below middle C of the keyboard are written in the bass (aka "C") clef.

Western Harmony Simplified   183

In the appendix examples to follow, middle C and the Cs an octave above and below middle C will be consistent reference points. Most of the notes in between these C notes will be labeled as well.

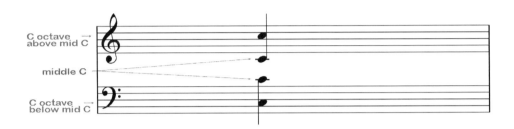

Notice below that there are two chords written out in staff notation form: C major and F major. In addition to the note labels, use the C note reference points. With enough practice, the notes in between the Cs will start to become familiar.

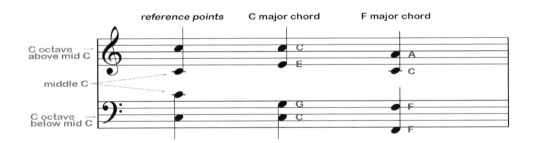

184 Western Harmony Simplified

Before moving on to the appendices, let's take a quick look at all of the notes as they appear on the staff. In the chord, notice the G 'under' the C an octave below middle C, also the E above the C an octave above middle C.

Also, in the labeling of the other notes, notice how some of the notes are on the lines and others are placed on the spaces. You might see that there is not much that visually connects the notes of the G and C clefs other than the middle C. It's best not to look for these connections.

This graphic is presented to give you an overall sense of the layout of the staff notes. **Don't worry about memorizing the labeling at this point. Mainly, use the C reference points.** As you work through the appendices, the labeling will start to make sense and become more intuitive.

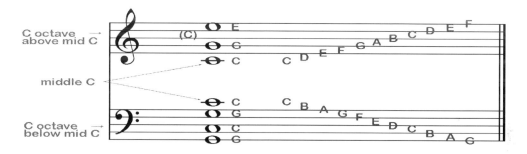

Now that you have some familiarity with the basic setup of staff notation, on to the the Appendices. Good Luck!

Western Harmony Simplified   **185**

Appendix 1
Formation of Triads

The C major chord written in the root position, in 'block' style appears as:

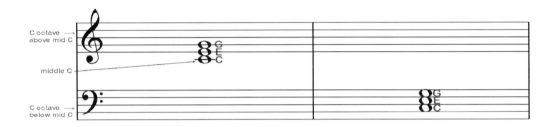

The Seven Diatonic Triads of C Major

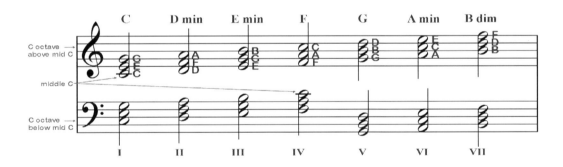

Chords are often played with voicings other than the above root positions. Here are four examples of open voicings for the C major chord:

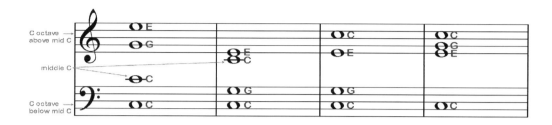

The root of the chord does not have to be the bass note. In the first example below, the G note (the 5th) of the C chord is in the bass; in the second example, the E note (3rd) of the chord is in the bass.

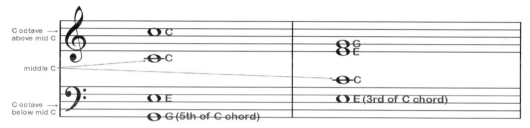

Below are examples of C major diatonic chords with the roots in the bass followed by voicings of the chords with the third or fifth in the bass:

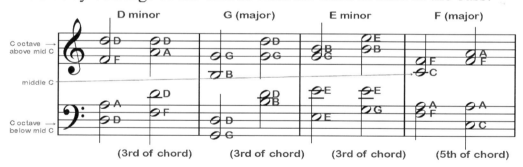

Triads in root, first and second positions:

Pianists typically practice triads (and later, seventh chords) in the basic block positions, starting with the root chord followed by the chord in the first position and second position. This approach helps in developing familiarity with the notes of the chords throughout the keyboard.

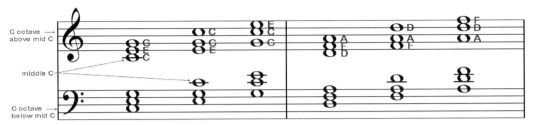

REVIEWING TRIADS

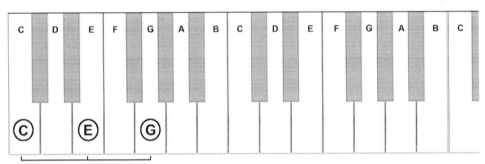

These three notes form
the C <u>major</u> chord

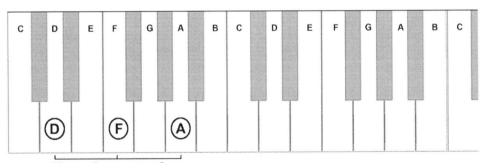

These three notes form
the D <u>minor</u> chord

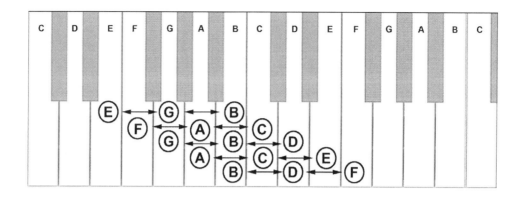

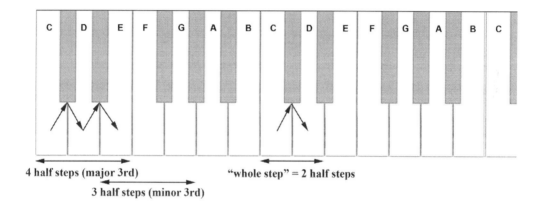

4 half steps (major 3rd)
3 half steps (minor 3rd)
"whole step" = 2 half steps

Western Harmony Simplified

Appendix 2
Voice Movement Between Triads

Notice that although there are three notes in a triad, the following examples use chords containing four notes. This will require that one of the three notes of the triad be played twice ("doubled"). Four notes are commonly used for building and "voicing" chords in classical and jazz as these notes are analogous to the bass, tenor, alto, and soprano voices derived from early choral music. In this first example, a C (I) chord moves to an F (IV) chord.

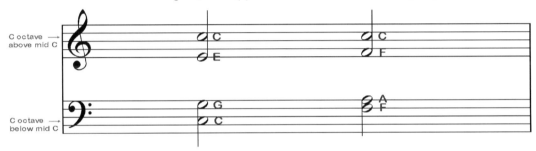

In the next example, a C (I) chord moves to an F (IV) chord followed by a D minor (II) chord, a G (V) chord and then back to the I chord C. Notice that in this progression, the root note of each chord is in the bass and this root note is the note that is doubled in the chord. (For example, the F chord is composed from the bottom up of F (the root of that chord), A, C, and again the root of the chord (F) as the top voice.)

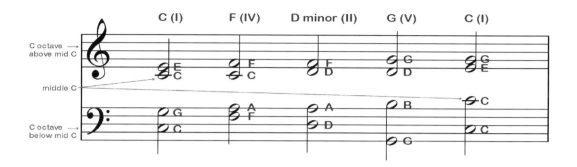

There are two very important things to notice in the above progression:

1) The individual voices (bass, tenor, alto, and soprano) move in a limited way, avoiding large intervallic leaps. In the move from the C to F chord, the top voice E of the C chord moves up a half step to the F note of the F chord, the C in the alto voice of the C chord stays the same as the chord changes to F, the G note tenor voice of the C chord moves a step up to the A of the F chord, and the bass note moves from C to F.

2) Each of the chords is spaced differently with respect to the individual notes - some are more open type chords and others are more closed (the F chord is more closed as its notes are as close to each other as is possible, whereas the G chord or at least part of it is quite open due to the large space between the G bass and B tenor voices.

Following is an example of an F chord voiced first in a closed position, then in an open position:

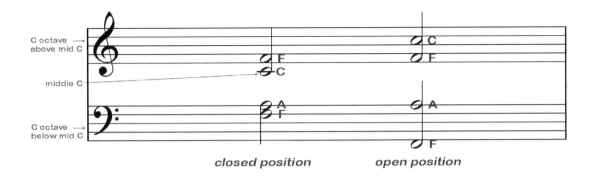

In the previous example, notice that in the open position chords there is a distance greater than an octave between the bass and tenor voices. This is acceptable between these voices, but it is generally not a good idea sonically to have a distance greater than an octave between the tenor and alto and alto and soprano voices.

EXERCISE:

Try writing some of these phrases using the diatonic chords in the key of C. Start and finish with the C (I) chord and move through three to five chords in between. Remember, try to avoid large intervallic leaps in the voices and for this exercise, the root of the chord should stay in the bass and be the doubled note. Once you feel somewhat comfortable composing these phrases, for the chords following and preceding the root position C chord, you can begin to use chords consisting of the third of the fifth in the bass.

Following is an example:

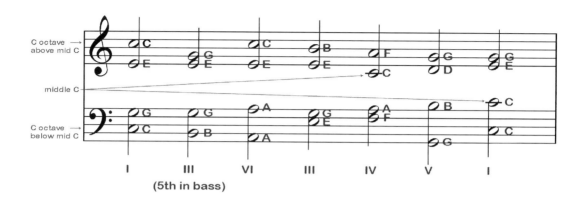

I strongly recommend spending time with these exercises. They are useful not only to acquaint yourself with the staff notes, but the work in voice leading and diatonic chords will serve to strengthen your harmonic and compositional capabilities. For now, use the limited instructions I have provided along with your ear to approach each phrase as a mini-composition. (In other words - make it sound good!)

Western Harmony Simplified

Appendix 3
Formation of Seventh Chords

The C major seven (Cmaj7) chord written in the root position, in 'block' style appears as:

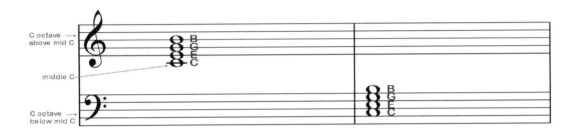

Diatonic Seventh Chords in the key of C major

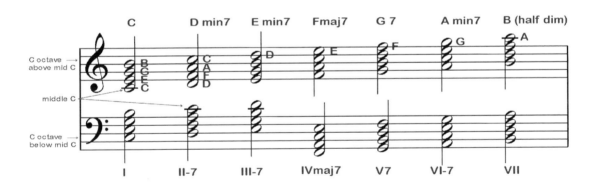

In the chords above, notice that the B, D and F notes of the G7 chord are also found in the B half diminished chord. Because of these shared common notes, the diminished chord (in this example: B diminished) is often viewed as essentially the same chord as the dominant chord containing the same notes (in this example: G7).

194   Western Harmony Simplified

As with triads, the seventh chords can be played using 'open' voicings.

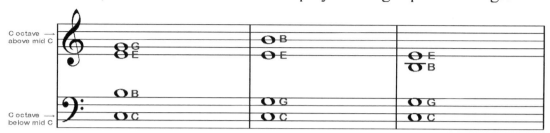

The root of the chord does not have to be the bass note. In the first example below, the G note (the 5th) of the chord is in the bass; in the second example, the E note (3rd) of the chord is in the bass.

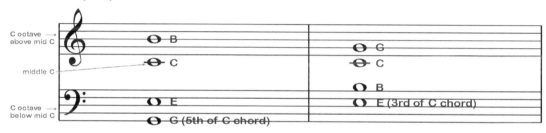

Following are examples of C major diatonic seventh chords with the roots in the bass followed by voicings of the chords with the third or fifth in the bass:

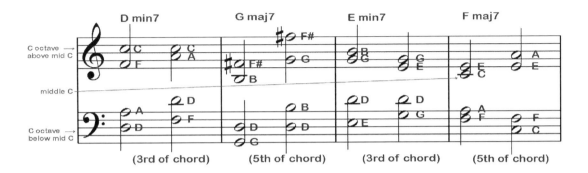

It is useful to be familiar in theory and in practice with the various block chord "inversions" of the seventh chords. Following is the root position and three inversion chords for C maj7 and A min7:

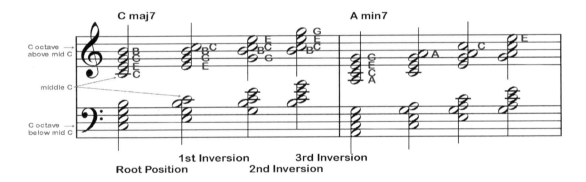

Chord voicings can be formed by combining open voicings with the chord inversions. The chords following contain both open intervals and block chord inversions (the inversions are bracketed).

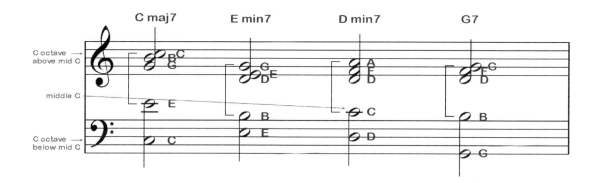

REVIEWING SEVENTH CHORDS

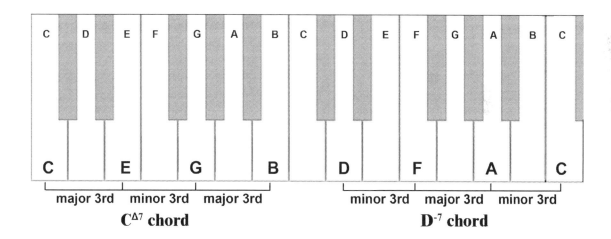

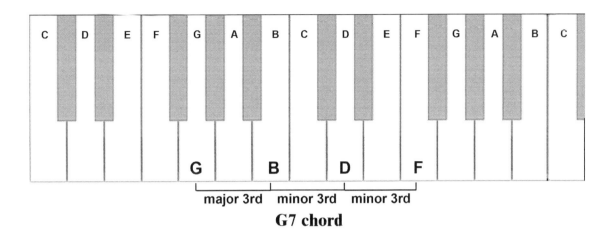

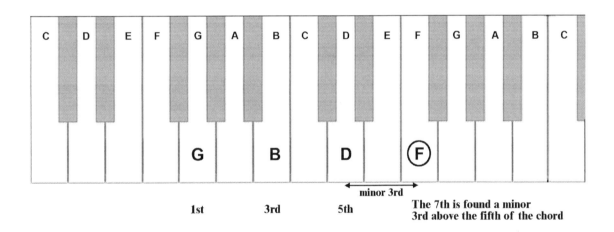

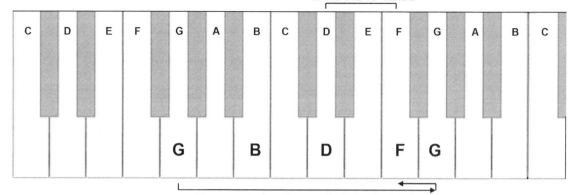

Western Harmony Simplified

Appendix 4
Voice Movement Between Seventh Chords

Many of the same exercise instructions we saw in the appendix Voice Movement Between Triads are to be applied to composing harmonic phrases with seventh chords. There are a few differences. First, using the four note seventh chord means that in a four-note chord, no notes will be repeated as they were using the triad. Also, as we have often seen, the seventh note of the chord has an intrinsic pull to the third of the following chords; the exercises should take note of this attraction and allow for this natural voice movement.

Below, we have an example of a G7 (V) chord moving to a C (I) chord. The G7 is voiced with the third of the chord in the bass. Notice the half step movement from the notes F to E in the top voice and B to C in then bottom voice.

EXERCISE:

Try composing phrases using diatonic seventh chords as well as triads. As with the triad exercises, start and finish the progression with the C (I) chord. Also as in the previous exercises, for now try to avoid large intervallic leaps from voice to voice. In the first example below, the roots of the chords are used in the bass except for the third to last chord C which contains the fifth in the bass. In the second example, there is a freer use of seventh chords and chords using the third in the bass. This opens up the sound. Notice that in the second example, the C chord towards the end is again written with the fifth in the bass. These last chords comprise a commonly used 'cadence' in classical music.

Below is a sequence that contains three seventh chords with the third in the bass. Notice that in the VI7 to II chord sequence, the VI functions as a V chord to the II (A7 to D minor). The III7 chord moves to a III minor7 chord prior to 'resolving' to the A minor VI chord.

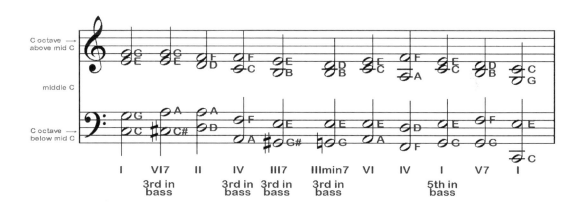

Western Harmony Simplified 201

In your phrases, start out simply by using four to eight chords in the sequence. Again, working on these voice movement exercises is highly recommended. Now that the seventh chord has been introduced, the creative possibilities expand, and you can start to work with the idea of V chords being used to lead to various chords within the diatonic system.

Appendix 5
Intervals

The graphic below outlines the intervals within an octave range:

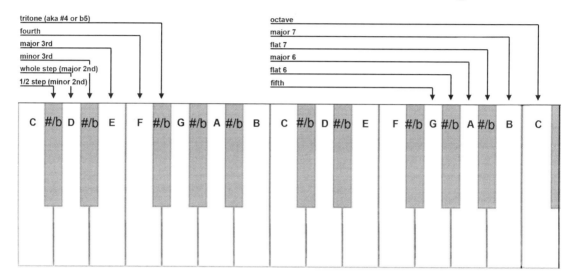

Intervals can be formed from any note. For example (below): an A note is an interval of a fifth above D; a G is a minor third above E. Conversely, G is an interval of a major third below B, and so forth.

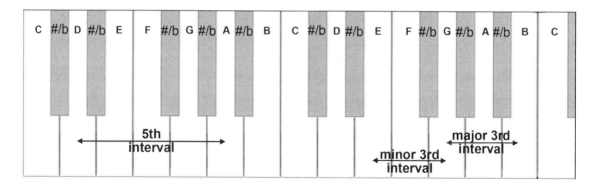

Western Harmony Simplified

Intervals in staff form

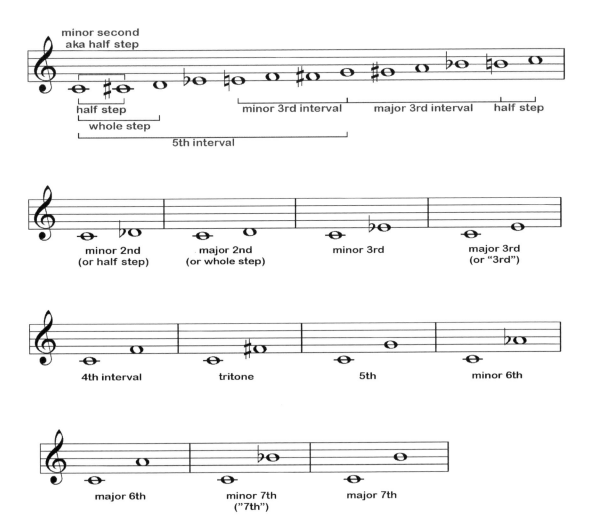

Intervals are determined in both directions. In the first bar above, the Db note is an interval of a minor 2nd away from C, and the C is an interval of a minor 2nd from Db. These interval directions are referred to as "ascending" and "descending." Again, note that the intervals can be formed starting on any notes. A is a fifth above D, G# is a major third above E, C is a fourth above G, etc...

| 5th | major 3rd | 4th interval | minor 2nd (or half step) |

Familiarity with intervals is essential for a thorough understanding and practice in music. As has been explained in the text, chord structure of individual chords is based on intervallic relationships. These graphics from the text exemplify how **intervals define the seventh chords.**

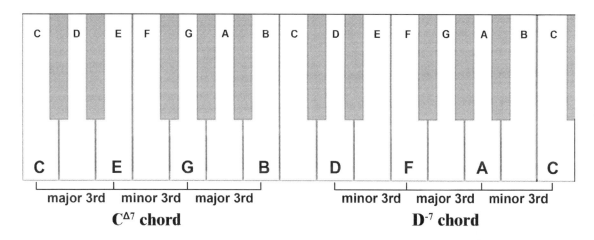

Western Harmony Simplified

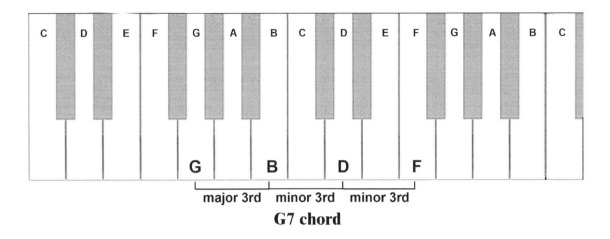

G7 chord

With practice, the intervals will become visually familiar on the keyboard. **Visual recognition** is one aspect of learning the intervals. Theoretical understanding also facilitates the process. A vital aspect of understanding and using intervals is being able to recognize intervals by way of the ear. A common exercise to strengthen the ear is to sing and memorize songs that employ the intervals. Below is a list of songs that applies to each interval. You can substitute your own songs.

Using Songs to Learn Intervals

Interval	Ascending	Descending
minor 2nd	Jaws	Jaws
major 2nd	Frere Jacques	Mary Had a Little Lamb
minor third	Impossible Dream	Star Spangled Banner
major third	From the Halls of Montezuma	Three Blind Mice
fourth	Taps	Working on the Railroad

tritone	Maria (West Side Story)	use Maria reversed
fifth	My Favorite Things	Feelings
minor 6th	Because (Beatles)	use Because reversed
major 6th	Chopin Nocturne (Eb)	Knowbody Knows ..
seventh	Somewhere (West Side Story)	Watermelon Man
major seventh	Don't Know Why (Nora Jones)	I Love You (Cole Porter)
octave	Somewhere Over the Rainbow	Willow Weep For Me

Appendix 6
Discretionary Dominant Chords and Other Substitutes

Discretionary dominant chords can be formed by substituting a dominant chord for the minor seven chords within a diatonic system.

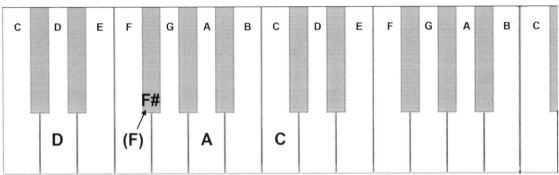

A II^{-7} chord becomes a II^7 chord by using a major third instead of a minor third

Below, the III and VI chords in the key of C major are turned into dominant chords by raising the third in the chord a half step. These substitutions provide for a more blues/jazz/r&b sound, and are also useful as a type of V chord (quasi-dominant) to a chord an interval a fifth below (for example: an E7, the III chord of C, leading to an A minor, the VI chord of C).

E-7 diatonic III chord   E7 discretionary dominant

This E-7 diatonic chord becomes an E7 and leads to the VI chord a fifth below (A-7)

208   Western Harmony Simplified

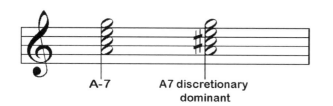

This A-7 diatonic chord becomes an A7 and leads to the II chord a fifth below (D-7)

DISCRETIONARY DOMINANT SUBSTITUTES

I	II	III	IV	V	VI	VII	(I)
C	D-	E-	F	G	A-	Bdim	C
CMaj7	D-7	E-7	Fmaj7	G7	A-7	B-7b5	C
	or	or		or	or	or	
	D7	E7		B-7b5	A7	G7	

Chords with common notes are also substituted for each other

The diatonic triads F and D minor share two common notes (F and A). Fmaj7 and Dmin7 share three common notes (F, A, and C). Similarly, C (and Cmaj7) share common notes with an E minor triad, and G7 shares common notes with a B diminished chord. These chord pairs are commonly substituted for the other.

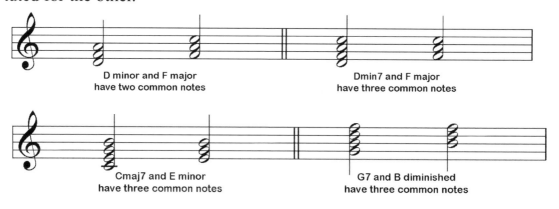

D minor and F major have two common notes

Dmin7 and F major have three common notes

Cmaj7 and E minor have three common notes

G7 and B diminished have three common notes

Western Harmony Simplified

Tritone Substitutions

In a tritone substitution chord, the third and seventh of the initial dominant chord become the seventh and third of the substitute chord.

IMPORTANT NOTE: notice that the 'B' note in the Db7 is written as a Cb. This is the same note, but it is more technically correct to write it as a Cb. In practice, this note will more commonly be written and perceived as a B.

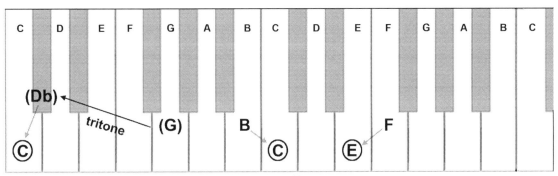

3rd and 7th of G⁷ become the 7th and 3rd of Db⁷ which can resolve to the C chord

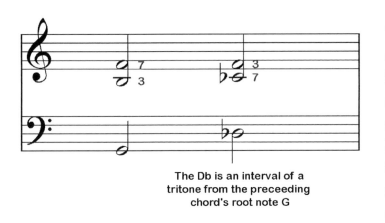

The Db is an interval of a tritone from the preceeding chord's root note G

Tritone substitution chords also can be used in place of the common discretionary dominant chords. In addition to Db7 substituting for the G7 V chord, Ab7 substitutes for D7 (the II chord), Eb7 substitutes for A7 (the VI chord), and Bb7 for E7 (the III chord). These discretionary dominant chords - the II, VI and III typically lead to their 'I' chords, a chord an interval of a fifth below. The tritone substitution chord is a half step (!) above the destination I chord. Accordingly:

G7 (Db7) resolves to   C
D7 (Ab)   —>   G
A7 (Eb7)   —>   Dmin
E7 (Bb7)   —>   Amin

Other Substitutions Related to Dominants, II Vs, Tritones, Sus Chords and Half-Step Resolutions

There are various ways players and composers can approach dominant chords. This also applies to the diatonic II, III, and VI chords (all minor), which are commonly changed into dominant chords and, therefore, can utilize similar substitutions. Below, I have charted some of the ways a simple G7 (V chord in the key of C) can be morphed into other chords and progressions.

G7
Gsus   (every V chord can be turned into a sus chord)
D- G7   (every V chord can become a II V)
D7 G7   (the II D minor chord is replaced with the discretionary dominant)
D7 Db7   (G7 is replaced by the tritone substitution Db7)
Ab7 Db7   (D7 is replaced by the tritone substitution)
Absus7 Gsus7   (dominant chords can be replaced with a sus chord)
Eb-7 Ab7 -> G7   (sus chords can be broken down into its component II V)

PLEASE NOTE THAT THIS CHART CAN WORK BACKWARD OR FORWARD STARTING WITH ANY OF THE CHORDS OR PROGRESSIONS. For example, a player might see a D- to G7 in the score and choose to play a GSUS OR G7 chord, OR alternatively, play one of the progressions from below it on the chart (i.e., D7 to Db7 or Absus7 to Gsus7).

Appendix 7
Formation of the Sus Chord

The basic sus (suspended) chord is formed by raising the 3rd of the major chord one half step. In the graphic below, The G chord containing the notes G, B, and D becomes G, C, and D.

The raised 3rd effectively becomes the 4th of the chord. (The B note becomes C.)

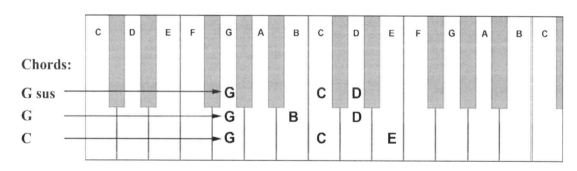

Sus chords are often played with more complex voicings than the one used in the above example. The example to the left shows two common sus chords

used in pop music and jazz/r&b/soul. The simplest way to think of these chords is as a Fmaj7 over G (Fmaj7/G) and a Dmin7 over G (D-7/G). Arrangers may designate chords as a sus chord, or a sus7 chord (i.e., Gsus7), or more specifically as an Fmaj7 or Dmin7 over G as in the ex-

Western Harmony Simplified   213

amples. In certain styles of music, chords designated as sus chords will more typically be played with one of these richer voicings to the left.

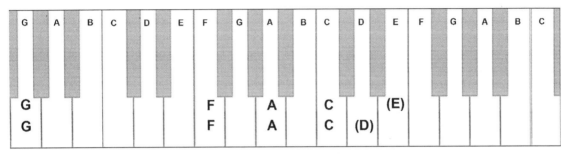

Various types of sus chords

SUS CHORD VOICING POSSIBILITIES BUILT ON THE V CHORD IN THE KEY OF C (Gsus/ Gsus7, F maj7/G, or D-7/G etc.)

In the potpourri of sus chord voicings that follow, notice that some of the voicings may not use all of the notes available as in the previously described voicings. Others may incorporate additional notes from the diatonic scale in order to create a more impressionistic type sound.

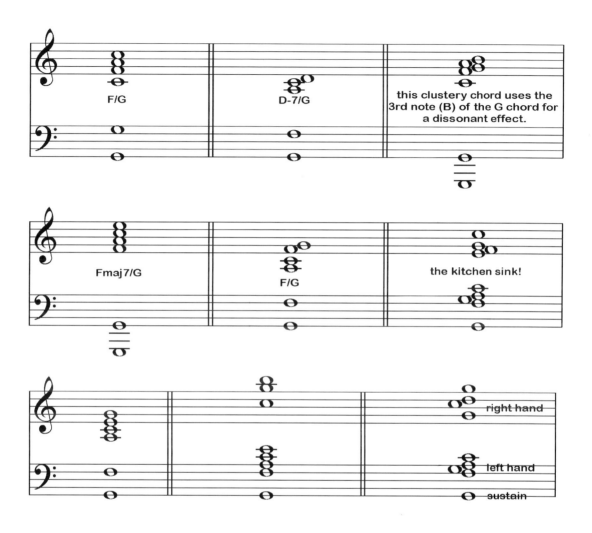

The B (the third) is used again in this chord. It creates a sharp edge for the otherwise soft and rich quality of the chord.

This chord is not as difficult to play on piano as it might appear. Use the pedal to sustain the low G and then play the remaining notes with the left and right hands.

Western Harmony Simplified

★★★★★★★★★★★★★★★★★★★★★★★

The more advanced sus chords reveal that the sus chord can be viewed as two chords 'rolled' into one. This idea is explored in more detail in the text. Essentially, the sus chord can be seen as a combination of a II and a V chord. It is easiest to understand this idea by looking at the D-7 over G. The G is the V chord to C and the D-7 is the II chord in the C major diatonic system. In effect, you have the II and V chord as one chord. Sus chords, as in the previous examples that do not contain the D-7, have a similar effect. The F major chord (the IV chord in the key of C) shares common notes with the D-7 chord and therefore has a similar sound and function.

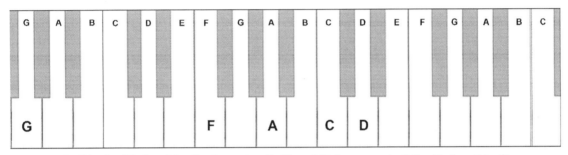

D-7 is the II chord in C; the notes G, F, and D form part of the V chord in C

Appendix 8
The Minor Diatonic System

The root of the minor key is an interval of a minor third below the root of its relative major key. A minor is the "relative minor" to C major, E minor the relative minor to G major, B minor the relative minor to D major, and so on. In this way, every major key has its relative minor, and every minor key has its relative major.

C Major Scale

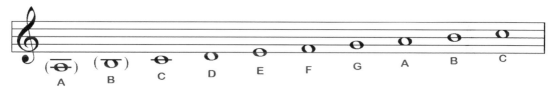

The "natural" minor scale uses the note material from its relative major scale.

A Minor Scale

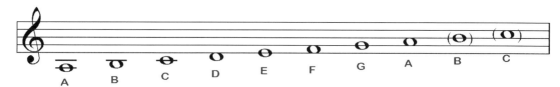

The three types of minor scales are the natural, harmonic, and melodic. Due to harmonic considerations (mainly the need for a major third in the V chord), in the harmonic minor scale, the seventh degree is raised. In the melodic minor scale the sixth and seventh degree are raised as the scale ascends.

Western Harmony Simplified

A Natural Minor Scale

A Harmonic Minor Scale

A Melodic Minor Scale

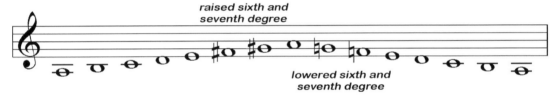

THE NATURAL MINOR SCALE AND ITS RELATED CHORDS

Just as the chords of the major diatonic system are derived from the major scale, the chords of the minor diatonic system are derived from the minor scale material. Because of the raised six and seven in the minor scales, there are various chord possibilities within the system.

Triads derived from the A natural minor scale

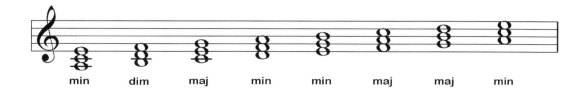

Seventh chords derived from the A natural minor scale

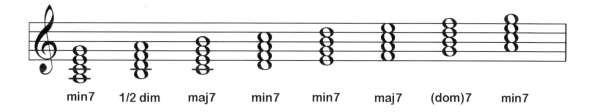

THE HARMONIC MINOR SCALE AND ITS RELATED CHORDS

Triads derived from the A harmonic minor scale (notice the use of the G#)

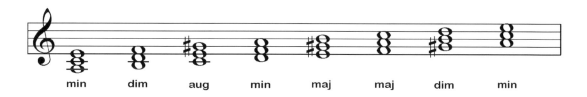

Seventh chords derived from the A harmonic minor scale

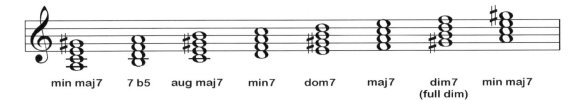

min maj7   7 b5   aug maj7   min7   dom7   maj7   dim7 (full dim)   min maj7

THE MELODIC MINOR SCALE AND ITS RELATED CHORDS

The descending part of this scale is the same as the natural minor

Triads derived from the A melodic minor scale (notice the use of the F# and G#)

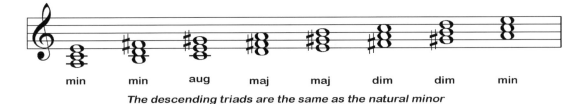

min   min   aug   maj   maj   dim   dim   min

The descending triads are the same as the natural minor

Seventh chords derived from the A melodic minor scale

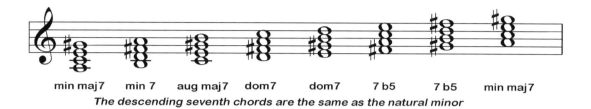

min maj7   min 7   aug maj7   dom7   dom7   7 b5   7 b5   min maj7

The descending seventh chords are the same as the natural minor

IMPORTANT NOTE:

Please do not get frustrated by or try to memorize all the previous chord combinations. The easiest approach is to familiarize yourself with the three minor scales. As this occurs, the chords will come naturally. Finally, the chords that apply to each of the scales are not necessarily mutually exclusive. Many songs and improvisers use chords from each of the scales. For example, it would be possible to use the dominant type D7 chord from the melodic minor scale followed by a the B-7b5 from the natural or harmonic minor scales. This is simply a matter of discretion, style, and taste. The minor diatonic system is very flexible in this way and provides an array of harmonic options.

REVIEWING THE MINOR SCALES

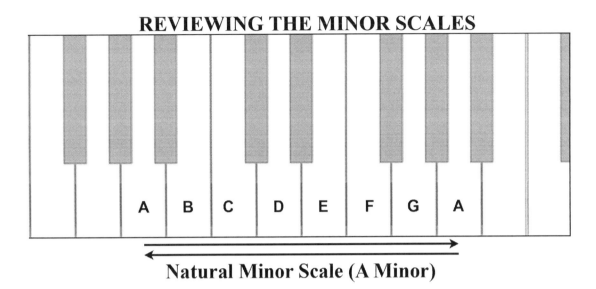

Natural Minor Scale (A Minor)

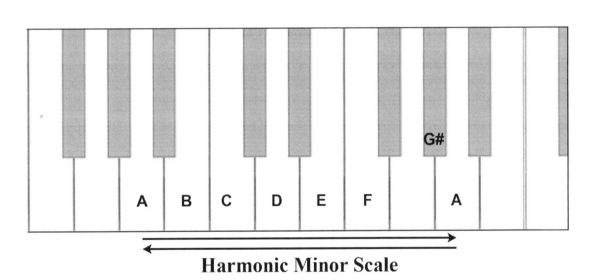

Harmonic Minor Scale

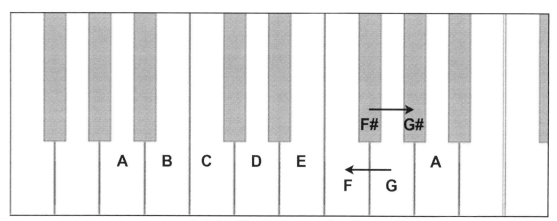

Melodic Minor Scale

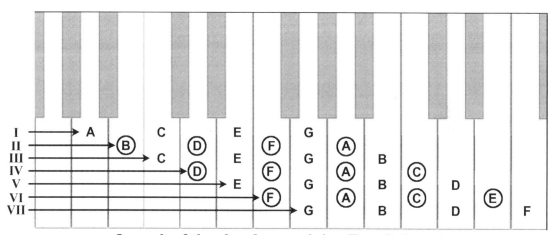

In each of the chords containing F or G there is a discretion to turn the F or G into an F# or G#. For example, the IV chord D-7 can be turned into a D7 (D F# A C).

Western Harmony Simplified

Appendix 9
Standard Jazz Voicings

You might not be surprised to learn that the foundation of the standard jazz voicing is the 3 7 (or 7 3). A solid understanding and familiarity with this voicing approach will make learning the more 'rich' voicings (those with more notes) easier.

The examples below show how the jazz voicings are used within the II V I progression. Later in this appendix, we'll see that these chords can be used individually, not necessarily as part of a progression.

Simple Voicing - using only the 3 and 7 of the chord

Intermediate Voicing - here, the 9 is added to the II chord, the 13 to the V chord, and the 9 to the I

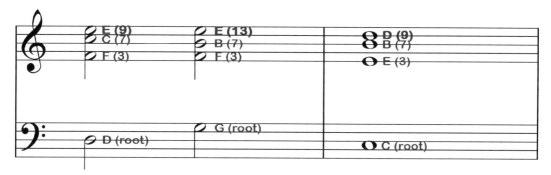

The Full Standard Jazz Voicing - notice that the 5th of the chord is added to the II and I chord, but not to the V chord

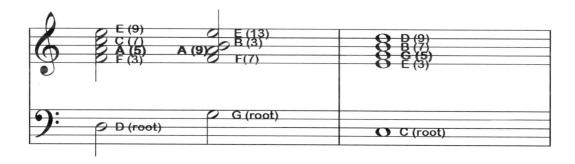

Depending on the chord color desired (which is often determined by where you are on the range of the keyboard), the above voicings can be played with the **order of notes reversed**. It's important to become familiar with both versions of these voicings.

Simple Voicing with 3 7 reversed

Intermediate Voicing reversed

226 Western Harmony Simplified

Full Voicing reversed

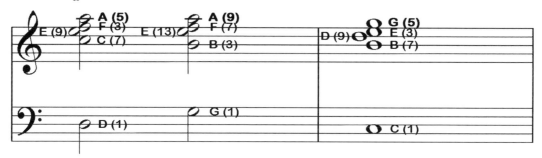

Below is the previous voicing an octave lower

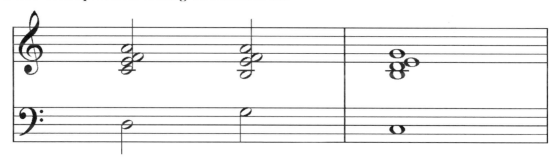

Following are simple 1 7 voicings used most often in the left hand as accompaniment to melodic improvisation (i.e. blues or bebop). They can also be used to support a richer jazz voicing the in the right hand.

Western Harmony Simplified

KEEP IN MIND - all of the standard jazz voicings can be played in the right or left hand, or split into both. The example below shows in the first chord D-7 a reversed full voicing divided between the left and right hand. Also notice how the left hand voicing by itself is the 1 7 voicing just described. The remaining two chords contain the full voicings; the B note in the G7 voicing could be played either in the left or right hand while the Cmaj7 chord uses the fifth of the chord (G) which adds richness.

THE MAJOR II V I VOICINGS IN ALL KEYS

On the following pages, the full standard jazz voicings are laid out in all keys for those wishing to do more advanced work. First, the full jazz standard voicings of the II V I progression are presented with the II chord voiced in the 3 5 7 9 position. The progressions are then presented in the commonly used 'reversed' position, that is, starting with the II chord voiced in 7 9 3 5 position. The II V I standard jazz voicings in the minor keys are not presented in this appendix. They follow a similar format to the major key voicings, but contain variations due to the three scales of the minor system.

The Dmin7 II chord voiced as 3 5 7 9

The Dmin7 II chord voiced as 3 5 7 9, the "reversed position"

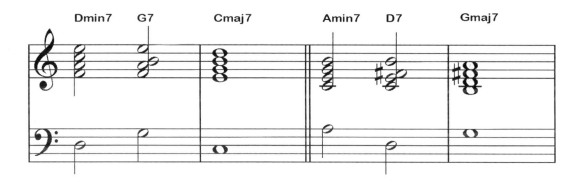

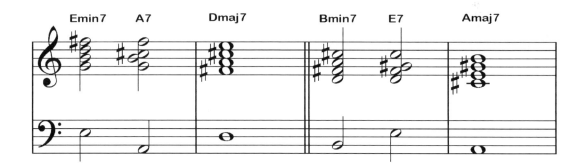

Western Harmony Simplified

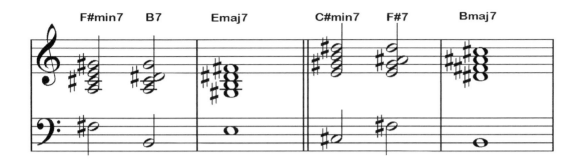

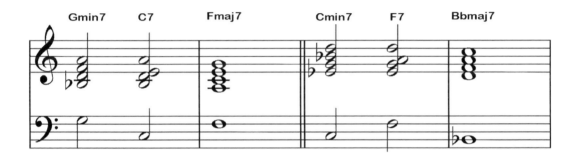

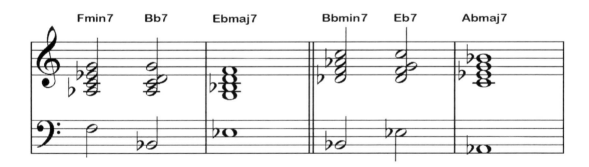

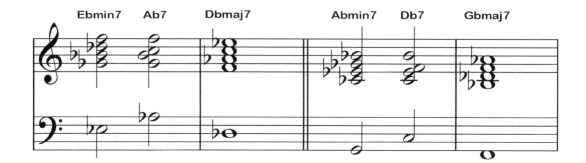

Reverse Position Voicings

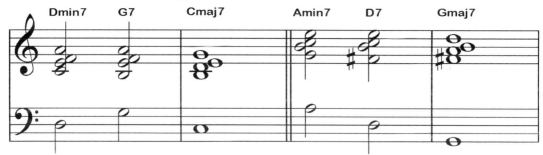

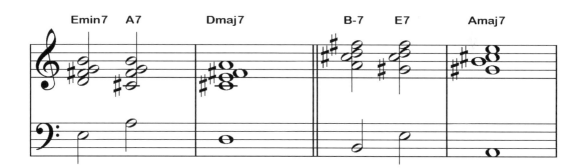

Western Harmony Simplified

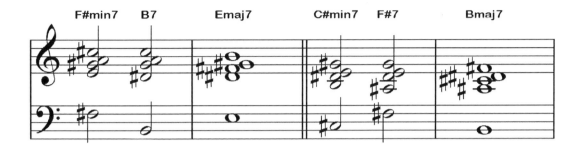
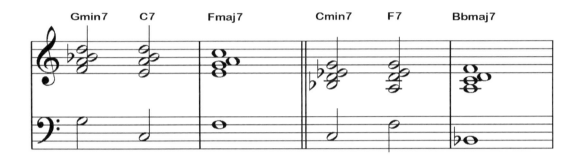
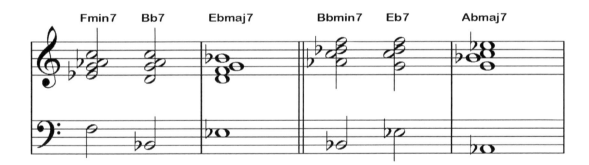

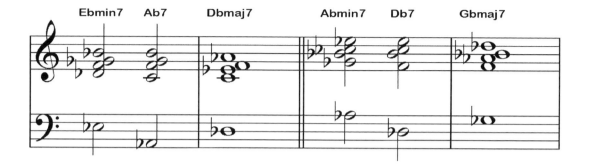

Playing through the II V I progressions is a useful way to practice the jazz voicings, particularly as you apply the voicings to new keys. The voicings for each of these chords within the progression, however, will also be useful in the context of chords that are not necessarily part of a II V I progression (for example: the G7 chord within a blues or vamp type of section, or a Fmaj7 to a Dmin7, the first two chords in the verse of Al Green's "Let's Stay Together").

Following are some examples of these 'individual' chords:

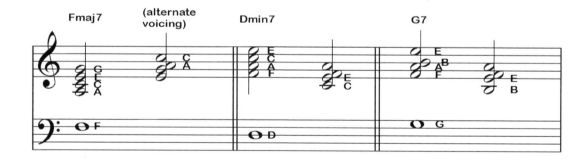

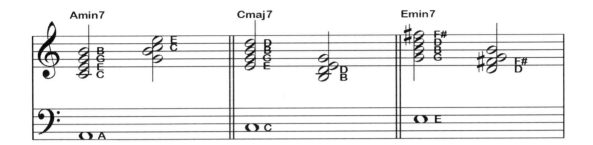

Appendix 10
Altered Jazz Chords

The diatonic scale provides the foundational material to build alterations of basic jazz chords.

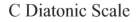

C Diatonic Scale

The V7 chord (G7) in the key of C derives its notes from the C major scale. The numbers 1, 3, 5, 7, and 9 in this context refer to the root of the G chord as being (1), the third of the G chord being 3, and so forth. This is an important numerical distinction to keep in mind when identifying and describing chord types.

G Mixolydian Scale (derived from the C major scale)

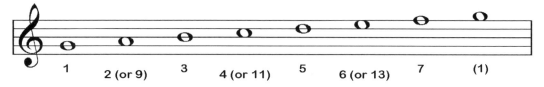

Western Harmony Simplified

Altered notes are formed by flatting or sharping notes within the scale of the given chord. Most typically, the 9 (2) and 13 (6) are flatted and the 11 is sharped. The 9th is also sharped in jazz and r&b/funk chording.

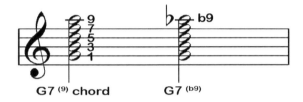

In this example, a diatonic $G7^9$ becomes a $G7^{b9}$ by flatting the 9th.

Care needs to be taken when voicing chords with extension notes. Chords are generally not voiced with contiguous notes as in the example above. Typically, the 5th of the chord is omitted.

Following are examples of altered jazz chord voicings with the root in the bass.

TENSION AND RELEASE

Altered chord tones are often resolved as a way to create a tension and release effect.

In this example, the flat 9 note Ab resolves by a half step to the G.

Following are additional examples of altered tones resolving to diatonic tones. In measure B, the sharp 9, the A# note in the sharp nine chord resolves by way of a half step to the ninth note A. In measure C, the sharp 9 resolves to the flat 9, and then to the chord root note G.

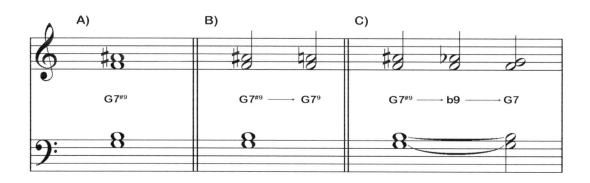

The flat 13 can also move to the note a whole step above. This does not quite feel like a full resolution. In the second measure, the F note is resolved a half step to the E of the C major chord, thus, completing a V7 to I progression.

Western Harmony Simplified

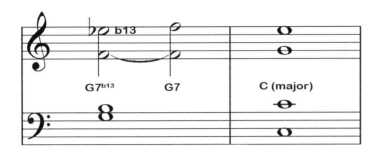

STANDARD JAZZ VOICINGS can be used as a template to add or substitute non-diatonic extension notes. Below, the G7 in each of the standard jazz voicing forms is followed by an altered version of the G7 chord.

Note that in the first example, the 13 appears beneath the 9 in the chord, yet it is noted in the chord description after the 9 (i.e., G7^{9,13}). It is more typical in the real world of chord notation to write the extensions starting with the lower number because it is simply easier to read. In some of the previous examples, extension notes have been written in the order which they appear in the chord (i.e., G7^{b13b9}). It was done this way simply as a pedagogic tool. Also, chords may be written this way if an arranger wants a chord to be played with a particular extension note as the top voice.

ADDITIONAL RICH ALTERED CHORD VOICINGS

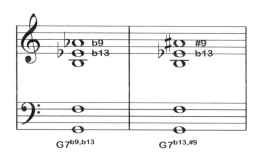

These examples incorporate more than one altered tone per chord.

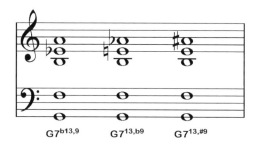

Chords can also use a combination of non-diatonic and diatonic extension notes.

RICHEST OF THE RICH (all the ingredients!)

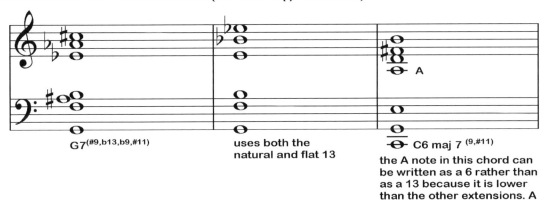

G7(#9,b13,b9,#11)

uses both the natural and flat 13

C6 maj 7 (9,#11)

the A note in this chord can be written as a 6 rather than as a 13 because it is lower than the other extensions. A 6th is more typically written with a Maj 7 chord than on dominant seventh chords.

Appendix 11 - The Blues

The C Blues Pentatonic Scale consists of five notes:

The 3rd and 5th intervals of the scale are the blue notes; the third can fall

somewhere on or between the minor third Eb and major third E; the fifth can fall somewhere on or between the G or the flat fifth Gb.

The Minor Blues generally does not use the major third E note in the blues scale

A C (major) blues can incorporate the blues scale starting on C and or the

Western Harmony Simplified

minor blues scale of its relative minor - A. 'Riffing' on the A minor blues scale while playing a C blues progression can produce a more country blues feel and open up additional colors.

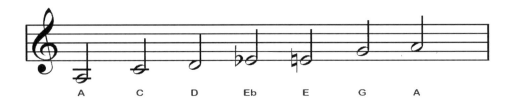

Left Hand Blues Accompaniment

ACCOMPANIMENT TO BASIC BLUES

VOICINGS APPLICABLE TO JAZZ INFLUENCED BLUES

These voicings use the 1 and 7 of each chord. Jazz piano greats Thelonious Monk and Bud Powell used these simple voicings.

These voicings use the 3 and 7 of each chord

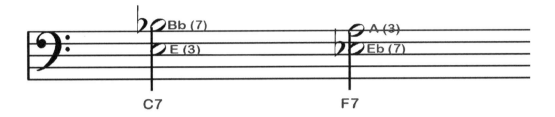

These voicings use the 3, 7 and 9 of C7 to the 7, 3 and 13 of F7

These voicings build on the previous with the addition of the the 13th into the C7 chord and the 9th into the F7 chord. These voicings can also be found in the Standard Jazz Voicings Appendix

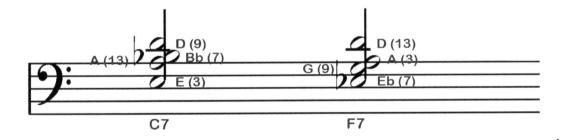

'Major' Blues

The chart below shows 12 ways to play the '12 bar blues,' the most common of the blues forms. Musicians playing rock, blues, jazz, r&b, and pop need to be familiar with this form. The progressions below reflect the most simple 'roots' style to the more complex chord layouts used in jazz. These progressions are in the key of C. Notice that these sequences are centered around the I, IV and V chords. Understanding this is very useful in order to have facility with the blues in all keys.

1	2	3	4	5	6	7	8	9	10	11	12
C7 (I)	C7	C7	C7	F7 (IV)	F7	C7 (I)	C7	G7 (V)	G7	C7 (I)	C7
C7	C7	C7	C7	F7	F7	C7	C7	G7	**F7**	C7	C7
C7	C7	C7	C7	F7	F7	C7	C7	G7	F7	C7	**G7**
C7	**F7**	C7	C7	F7	F7	C7	C7	G7	F7	C7	G7
C7	F7	C7	C7	F7	F7	C7	**A7**	**D7**	G7	C7	G7
C7	F7	C7	C7	F7	F7	C7	A7	D7	G7	C7	**D7 G7**
C7	F7	C7	**G-7 C7**	F7	F7	C7	**Bb7 A7**	D7	G7	**C7 A7**	D7 G7
C7	F7	C7	G-7 C7	F7	F7	**C7 B7**	Bb7 A7	D7	G7	C7 A7	D7 G7
C7	F7	C7	G-7 C7	F7	**F#°**	**C7 F7**	**E7 A7**	D7	G7	C7 A7	D7 G7
C7 C7/E	**F7 F#°**	**C/G Ab7**	**G7 F#7**	F7	**Bb7**	**E7**	A7	D7	G7	C7 A7	D7 G7
C7 C7/E	F7 F#°	C/G Ab7	G-7 C7	F7	Bb7	C7	A7	D7	G7	**C7 Eb7**	D7 G7
Csus7	**Csus7**	**Csus7**	**C7#9**	**Fsus7**	**Fsus7**	**Csus7 Bsus7**	**Bbsus7 Asus7**	**Ab7**	G7	C7 Eb7	D7 G7

There are blues forms outside of the 12 bar blues. Vamps are common – a repeated bass and guitar riff that might release to a different section (Tobacco Road performed by Edgar Winter, Peggy Lee's "Fever," and Muddy Waters' "I'm a Man" are good examples). These songs tend to be driven by the bass/guitar riff and the power of the blues melody (mostly derived from the blues scale).

Minor Blues

A minor blues is a common form used in jazz, but it has also been used at least in part in pop music. Van Morrison's "Moon Dance" is an example of the latter, so is Pink's more riff driven "Get the Party Started". The minor blues can use a similar structure to the blues outlined on the previous page. The examples below are based on an A minor blues. These examples get more complex throughout the chart – see if you can recognize substitutions base on some of the topics we have covered, i.e., every chord has its V chord, discretionary dominants, tritone substitutions, sus chords, dominants into II Vs, II Vs into dominants. . .

A-7 (I)	A-7	A-7	A-7	D-7 (IV)	D-7	A-7 (I)	A-7	E7 (V)	E7	A-7 (I)	A-7
A-7	A-7	A-7	A-7	D-7	D-7	A-7	A-7	E7	**D-7**	A-7	A-7
A-7	A-7	A-7	A-7	D-7	D-7	A-7	A-7	E7	D-7	A-7	**E7**
A-7	**D-7**	A-7	A-7	D-7	D-7	A-7	A-7	E7	D-7	A-7	E7
A-7	D-7	A-7	**A7b9, b13**	D-7	D-7	A-7	A-7	E7	D-7	A-7	E7
A-7	D-7	A-7	A7b9, b13	D-7	D-7	A-7	**C7**	**B-7b5**	E7	A-7	E7
A-7	D-7	A-7	**E-7b5** **A7**	D-7	D-7	A-7	**G-7** **C7**	**B7**	E7	**A-7** **C7**	**B-7b5** **E7**
A-7	D-7	A-7	E-7b5 A7	**D-7** **D-7/C**	**B-7b5** **E7**	**A-7** **Ab7**	**G-7** **F#7**	**FΔ7**	E7	A-7 C7	B-7b5 E7
A-7	D-7	A-7	E-7b5 A7	D-7 D-7/C	B-7b5 E7	A-7 Ab7	G-7 C7	**B-7,9,11**	**Bb7** **9, #11**	A-7 C7	**B-7,9,11** **E7**
A-7	D-7	A-7	E-7b5 A7	D-7 D-7/C	B-7b5 E7	A-7 Ab7	G-7 C7	B-7,9,11	Bb7 9, #11	**D7**	E7
A-7	A-7	A-7	A-7	D-7	D-7	A-7	A-7	**D7**	**C7**	**F7**	E7
A-7	D-7	A-7	**Asus7** **Eb7**	D-7	**Gsus7** **E7**	A-7	**Csus7**	**F7**	E7	A-7	E7

Western Harmony Simplified

In the minor blues, the I and IV chords are often colored with the 9 of the chord in cluster form. In the case of A-7, the chord could be voiced with G below middle up to a B, C and E (one of the standard jazz voicings). The V7 chord often is played with a sharp nine and/or a b13. The chords on jazz and pop charts are often not fully designated; it is presumed that the player will fill in the appropriate colors. Playing some of the progressions above without these added colors can sound awkward or incomplete. Once you are familiar with the standard jazz voicings, these progressions will start to fall into place.

How notes in the blues scale relate to the blues progression:

As discussed in the chapter, the way a note of the blues scale 'sits' against a chord has a powerful effect; the better blues and jazz musicians understand and work this well. Below are two examples of how powerful even one note of the blues scale can be when worked against the blues progression

Let's assume an Eb note will be repeated against the following blues progression.

The results are described below each chord.:

with Eb note

C7	F7	C7	C7	F7	F7	C7	A7	D7	G7	C7	G7
Eb is the #9	Eb is the 7	#9	#9	7	7	#9	Eb is the #11	b9	b13	#9	b13

248 Western Harmony Simplified

Here, let's assume a C note will be repeated against this blues progression. The results are described below each chord:

with C note

C7 C7/E	F7 F#°	C/G Ab7	G-7 C7	F7	Bb7	C7	A7	D7	G7	C7 Eb7	D7 G7
C is the 1 of each chord	C is the 5th of F7 and the diminished 5th of F#°	1 of first chord, 3 of Ab7	11, 1	5	9	1	#9	7	11	1, 13	7, 11

If two or three notes are used in a repetitive rhythmic figure (as in the previously mentioned Ellington piece "C jam blues"), blues based compositions and material for improvisation can easily be constructed. The lesson for blues and jazz improvisers – you don't need to play a lot of notes to make your point – keep it simple unless inspiration dictates otherwise!

Western Harmony Simplified

Appendix 12
MODES

The seven modes derived from the C major scale (Notice that the Aeolian mode is the A *natural* minor scale)

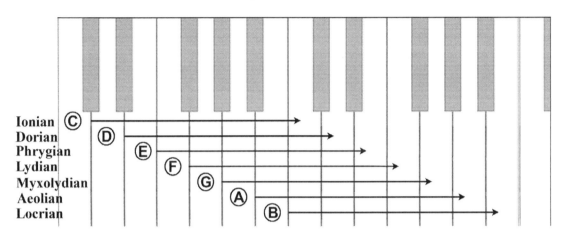

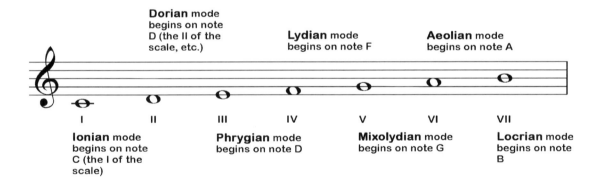

The seven modes can be formed out of any of the 12 major keys. The modes derived from the key of G are noted below.

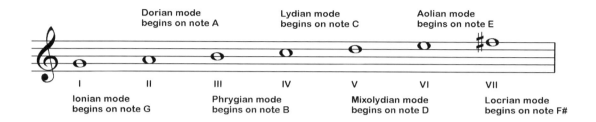

Notice that in the above two examples (and in all other keys), the Ionian scale is constructed from starting on the first degree of the major scale, the Dorian from the second degree, the Phrygian from the third degree, and so forth.

USING MODES TO FORM CLUSTER CHORDS

Notes within any major key can be added to chords as splashes of color. Below is a C major chord flavored with notes from the C major scale. The notes in the second chord, D and A, can be understood as an added 2 (or 9) and a 6 (or 13). More relevant to this lesson, these notes can be understood as being derived from the major scale. In this way, adding tones to chords can be less of an intellectual exercise and more about using scales and modes as a tonal palette.

Western Harmony Simplified

Notes from the C major scale can be added to any of the key's diatonic chords. Below is an F major chord (the IV chord within C major) with added notes from the C major scale source. This chord can be seen as being derived from an F Lydian scale, or from the C major scale source; either way, the result is the same.

This chord from the previous example is considered a cluster chord because of the proximity of the notes. The G and B are the 2 (or 9) and #11 of the F chord.

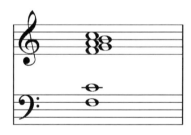

Here is the above chord voiced for two hands. This voicing produces a chord textured with both a clustered and open sound.

Clusters derived from the major source scale (or the associated mode) can be incorporated to supplement the standard jazz voicings. Below is a standard jazz voicing of Dmin7 followed by the same voicing with clusters added.

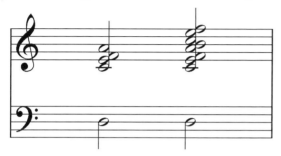

Below is a C major 7 chord spiced with notes derived from the C major scale. **ALERT!!** Notice that there is a non-diatonic F# note in this chord. Keeping it simple - - the 4th (or 11th) of the Cmaj7, or for that matter, any major 7 chord, is generally considered an "avoid note." When clustering a major seven chord, the 4th (11th) is commonly sharped. This is a slight anomaly from the simplicity of using modes to form chords. Depending on taste and context, the 4th note is generally available when forming minor seven, half-diminished, and even dominant chords.

A C maj7$^{(9,\#11,13)}$ chord, or thinking modally, a C major seven chord with notes added from the C major scale system (in this case, the F# note is a non-diatonic exception)

Western Harmony Simplified   253

Appendix 13
Diminished and Augmented Chords and Scales

The VII chord in the major diatonic system is a diminished chord. It is comprised of two minor third intervals.

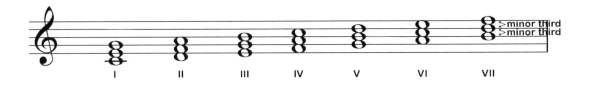

This diminished chord (and diminished chords in general) often function as the top three notes of a dominant seventh chord. Here, the B diminished VII chord is connected with the G7 V chord.

This diminished chord has the same tendency as the seventh chord to lead to the I chord (C). (The B note pulls to the C and the F note to the E.)

The B diminished chord also serves as the II chord in C major's relative minor key (A minor).

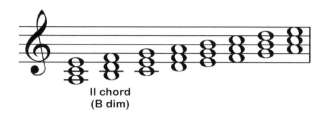

II chord
(B dim)

DIMINISHED SEVENTH CHORDS

The diminished chord on the VIIth degree of the major scale can also be turned into a seventh chord by adding the diatonic note a third above. The result is:

This chord is referred to as a *half diminished* chord because the interval between the 5th and 7th is a major third, not the minor third that defines the diminished triads. This chord is also referred to as a *Xmin7^{b5}*, a terminology more typical to the jazz idiom and commonly used to define the II chord in the minor key.

Diatonic seventh chords derived from the natural minor scale

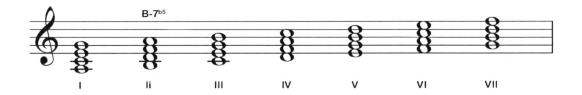

MORE ON THE DIMINISHED CHORD, THE AUGMENTED CHORD, RELATED SCALES, AND THE "VAGRANT" CHORD

The fully diminished chord (all notes separated by intervals of a minor third), and the augmented chord (all notes separated by intervals of a major third), share common characteristics.

The consecutive notes in the full diminished chord are each separated by a minor third interval.

The consecutive notes in the augmented chord are each separated by a major third interval.

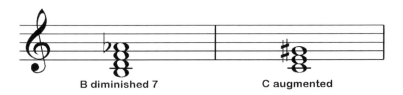

As described in the text, the symmetrical structure of the diminished and augmented chords creates an ambiguity as to the root of the chord, and therefore allows the chords to be used in a variety of harmonic contexts. Because of this characteristic, Schoenberg referred to these chords as "vagrants."

This diminished chord could be seen as the the upper structure of G7, Bb7 Db7, or E7 (all b9 chords) and could be used to modulate to C or (C minor), Eb, Gb, or A.

This augmented chord could be seen as a V type chord starting on either C, E or G# (Ab) and could be used to modulate to F, A, or C# (Db).

There are a total of three diminished chords and four augmented chords. The first three diminished chords below are repeated in different inversions.

Three diminished chords

Four augmented chords

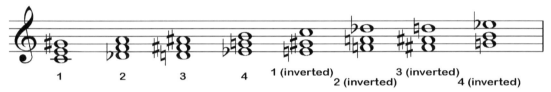

DIMINISHED AND AUGMENTED SCALES

There are three diminished scales and two augmented scales. The diminished scale is formed by alternating half steps and whole steps The augmented scale, also commonly known as the whole tone scale, is constructed of whole tone intervals.

Three diminished scales

Two whole-tone scales

Notice that whatever note you choose as the starting note of the whole tone scale, the resulting scale will contain the sequential notes in one of the two whole-tone scales above. Similarly, whichever note is chose as the starting note of a diminished scale, the resulting scale will contain the sequential notes of one of the three diminshed scales above.

Appendix 14
Polychords and Pedal Points

Creative Possibilites

As noted in the text, the **Polychord** is formed by the juxtaposition of two chords, typically triads or seventh chords. A simple example is a G triad placed over a C triad

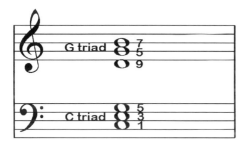

This chord can be viewed as a G triad over C triad, but notice that the resultant chord contains the notes comprising a Cmaj7$^{(9)}$ chord. Polychords can be used as a shortcut, or as another way to visualize chords with diatonic or non-diatonic extension notes.

In example 11-20 from the text, a diatonic polychord within the key of C major is built from the chords E minor and Dmin7. The resultant chord is a Dmin7$^{(9,11,13)}$

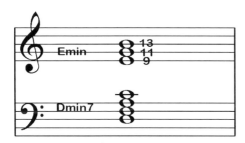

Western Harmony Simplified

The example, D triad of over a Cmaj7 uses a non-diatonic extension note (F#). The resulting chord is a Cmaj7$^{(9,\#11,13)}$.

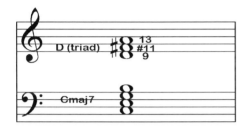

A more complex chord follows below: a Gb triad over a C7 chord. The resulting chord is a C7$^{(b9,\#11)}$

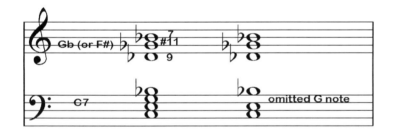

Typically, the G note in the C7 chord would be omitted to create a more open sounding chord, and to relieve some of the dissonance.

A **Pedal Point** is a repeated note or chord that is stationary as other notes or chords move around it. The pedal point is most often sounded either in the low or high register.

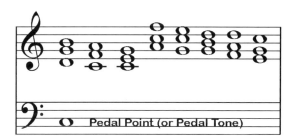

Here, the bass note C anchors the chords G, F, C and D minor. The Van Halen song "Jump" used this type of pedal point progression.

Non-diatonic chords can be used against pedal tones. In the example below, the descending triads are attracted to the following triads by way of half-step resolutions. Additionally, the chords are attracted to the C root

Here, the C note in the bass register serves as a pedal tone to the chords E, Eb, D, and Db.

Western Harmony Simplified

Another common use of a pedal tone is to play the root of the V chord to suspend a chord sequence. Here, in the key of C, the G note is used as a pedal point through a I VI II V I progression.

This progression can also be pedaled with a G note in the high register for a different effect (think high orchestral strings pedaling as woodwinds move through the chord sequence).

There is an interrelationship between polychords and pedal points. Viewed flexibly, a bass pedal point can be heard as the root of a chord (in the example below, a C chord). Accordingly, the sequence G/C, F/C, etc can be seen as a series of chords moving over a pedal point, but it can also be seen as a series of chords over an implied C chord.

Made in the USA
Lexington, KY
19 February 2015